D0651475

a special gift for

_____

with love,

_____

date

_____

Stories, sayings, and scriptures to Encourage and Inspire

hugs®

for Granddaughters

CHRYS HOWARD
Personalized Scriptures by
LEANN WEISS

HOWARD BOOKS
A DIVISION OF SIMON & SCHUSTER
New York   London   Toronto   Sydney

This book is dedicated to my
five precious granddaughters,

*Sadie, Macy, Ally,
Aslyn, and Bella.*

I love you more
than words can express
and enjoy every minute
I share with you!
May the Lord bless you
and keep you safe.

Love, 2-Mama

Our purpose at Howard Books is to:

- Increase faith in the hearts of growing Christians
- Inspire holiness in the lives of believers
- Instill hope in the hearts of struggling people everywhere

Because He's coming again!

Published by Howard Books, a division of Simon & Schuster, Inc.
1230 Avenue of the Americas, New York, NY 10020
www.howardpublishing.com

HOWARD
BOOKS

Hugs for Granddaughters © 2005 by Chrys Howard

All rights reserved, including the right to reproduce this book or portions thereof in any form whatsoever. For information, address Howard Subsidiary Rights Department, 1230 Avenue of the Americas, New York, NY 10020.

Library of Congress Cataloging-in-Publication Data
Howard, Chrys, 1953–
    Hugs for granddaughters : stories, sayings, and scriptures to encourage and inspire /
Chrys Howard ; personalized scriptures by LeAnn Weiss.
        p. cm.
    1. Granddaughters—Religious life. 2. Grandparent and child—Religious
aspects—Christianity. I. Weiss, LeAnn. II. Title.
BV4571.3.H69 2005
242'.643—dc22
                                                                        2004054125
ISBN-13: 978-1-4165-3374-0
ISBN-10:   1-4165-3374-5
12 11 10 9 8 7 6 5 4 3

HOWARD and colophon are registered trademarks of Simon & Schuster, Inc.

Manufactured in the United States of America

Paraphrased scriptures © 2005 by LeAnn Weiss
3006 Brandywine Dr.; Orlando, FL 32806; 407-898-4410

For information regarding special discounts for bulk purchases, please contact: Simon & Schuster Special Sales at 1-800-456-6798 or business@simonandschuster.com.

Edited by Between the Lines
Interior design by Stephanie D. Walker
Photography by Chrys Howard

Contents

*Grandchildren are the
dots that connect
the lines from generation
to generation.*

Lois Wyse

Making
Life Fun

Chapter One

Enjoying life is a gift from Me to you. Let Me keep you occupied with a glad heart. Even before you were born, I thought countless precious thoughts of you and ordained all of your days. My love is always before you.

Smiling on you,
Your God of Life

—from Ecclesiastes 5:19–20; Psalms 139:16–17; 26:3

When you were born, your grandparents felt as though the world had stopped spinning. Busy schedules came to a sudden halt. Cameras flashed, tears flowed, and hands reached out to take their turn holding you. An actress making her debut on the red carpet wouldn't get more devoted attention than you did on your opening day! You were the center of their world.

Even today, the expression "wrapped around your little finger" doesn't begin to describe how important, how special, how much fun you are and always will be to your grandparents.

You see, somewhere along the way, before
you came along, life had distracted them from the
fun of picking a four-leaf clover or jumping into a
swimming pool or riding a bike with no hands. But
that's where a granddaughter comes in. You remind
them how much fun life can be.

There's more to it than just the activities you share
with them. Knowing how much you love them
makes life more enjoyable. Your phone calls or
e-mails are the best part of their day. And no
matter how tired or how busy your grandparents are, they're always up for the special
fun only a granddaughter can bring.

What a grand thing
it is to be loved!
What a far grander
thing it is to love!

Victor Hugo

Joanne had a hard time saying no to seeing her grandchildren, but the evening proved to be more of a challenge than she had anticipated.

acts of love

Joanne rushed around the kitchen trying to get a hurried pot of meat sauce on the stove before her husband got home. She didn't always try to have supper on time—they had grown accustomed to eating out after work. But tonight she had so much to do at home that she had left work early and told her husband, Jim, that she might as well put something on for the two of them. After teaching school for many years, she loved the fact that her new schedule could be more flexible. Still, the bookkeeping responsibilities for their family-owned hardware store now rested heavily on her shoulders, and it seemed no matter how much she accomplished at the office, there was always more to do after working hours.

I don't know if I should be thankful for computers or angry they were ever invented, she thought as she looked at the laptop resting on the kitchen table, waiting for her to begin the night's work.

"Don't look at me like that!" Joanne warned the beckoning computer. "I have to finish supper, bake a cake, work on my Sunday-school lesson, clean the house, and wash a load of clothes before you even get opened." She smiled at herself for talking to a machine as she dumped a can of tomato sauce over the browned ground sausage.

The sudden musical tones from her cell phone startled her out of her harried concentration. She wiped her hands and fumbled through the clutter in her purse to retrieve the phone.

"Hello," she answered, trying not to sound like the interruption was unwelcome.

"Mimi?" said a faint little voice on the other end of the line.

"Sissy, is that you?" Joanne asked, knowing it was her seven-year-old granddaughter.

"It's me!" Sissy said, louder and more confident now that she knew she had dialed the right number.

"Hi, sweetheart, what are you doing?" Joanne asked, trying to hold the phone with her chin and shoulder while grabbing a cake mix from the pantry.

"Can I spend the night? Can I?" Sissy asked in her sweetest tone—the one that rarely received a negative reply.

But this was a night Joanne had over committed herself already. Not wanting to turn her down directly, she decided to take another approach. "Sissy, Mimi has to bake a cake for Mrs. Potter, who is sick, and take it to her house."

"I don't care," came the quick reply.

"Sissy, Mimi has to get the house cleaned and the clothes washed, because tomorrow night after work, I'm having company for dinner," Joanne tried again, wondering briefly why she always talked to her granddaughter in third person.

The sweet little voice came back undaunted. "I don't care."

Joanne offered one last excuse. "You know it's a school night, and you'll have to get in bed pretty early."

"I don't care."

She had met her match. Joanne smiled and at last gave in as she thought of Sissy's toothless grin and deep dimples. "Well, it's a date then. Go get Mommy and let me see if she'll bring you over."

"Hang on, I'll go get her!" Sissy said. Joanne imagined Sissy's brown ponytail bouncing with each step as she ran to find her mom.

As she'd been talking to Sissy, Joanne had poured the mix in to the bowl and added the water and three eggs. Now she started the mixer, knowing she couldn't spare one minute waiting for her daughter to come to the phone. Her mind was racing, knowing that having Sissy would add to her already busy evening. She didn't really mind. Sissy wasn't any trouble. She just wanted to be able to spend some quality time with her, and tonight's schedule didn't leave much room for that.

"Mom, can you hear me?" Joanne's daughter was yelling into the phone over the whirring of the mixer.

"Oh, I'm sorry, Melanie. I was mixing a cake while Sissy was getting you. I've got to get this in the oven for Sandy. She's just home from the hospital."

"That's OK. Mom, I didn't know Sissy was calling you. Now that she's memorized your cell-phone number, you'll have to tell her no sometimes. You know she'd sleep over there every night if we'd let her."

Joanne smiled at her daughter's warning.

"It's OK, Melanie, she's never any trouble. I just don't like it when I can't relax and enjoy being with her. I've got a pretty full schedule tonight, but she's welcome to come whenever you can bring her." Joanne licked off a bit of cake mix that had landed on her knuckle.

"Actually, I was about to leave the house to pick up some milk, so I'll bring her right over. Are you sure you don't mind?"

"Of course I don't mind. See you soon."

Joanne had made so many cakes in her life, she could do it blindfolded. It only took a few minutes to spray the pan, pour in the batter, and shut the oven door. *Now to the laundry*, she thought as she washed her hands. But again the phone rang.

"Hey, Momma." Joanne's youngest daughter was on the line.

"Hi, babe, did you have a good day?" Joanne asked, knowing Rebecca's day involved two toddlers, and the answer could easily be no.

"Pretty good. The kids actually took naps at the same time. Can you believe it?"

"Now that is a good day! I used to love it when you and your sister napped at the same time. I thought I was on vacation!"

"Mom, I know this is short notice," Rebecca said sheepishly, "but I need some help with the kids tonight."

"What's going on?" Joanne asked.

"Remember my friend, Amy? She had her baby today, and I really need to go see her. Her mom can't come until the weekend. I won't be gone long."

"I'm really busy tonight, but if you can deliver a cake to Sandy's house for me on your way back home, I guess I can watch them for a little while." Joanne had a hard time saying no to seeing any of her grandchildren.

"Thanks, Mom. You're the best. I'll be there in about thirty minutes."

Joanne stirred the meat sauce one more time and went to collect the laundry. Hurrying back to the bathroom, she wondered where all that extra time was that she thought she'd have when the kids were grown. "Why can't Jim use a towel more than one time? My laundry duties would be cut in half if I could get that man to use a towel twice before throwing it on the floor. Oh well, you can't teach an old dog . . ." Joanne realized she was mumbling and shook her head as she gathered an armload of towels.

With the laundry started, Joanne returned to the kitchen. She opened the door of the refrigerator and then forgot why she had opened it.

Remembering it was the noodles she really wanted, she closed the refrigerator and headed for the pantry, thinking about an article she had read the night before about memory loss. *I should be cooking the foods mentioned in that article that would help my memory . . . if I could remember what they were,* she mused as she retrieved the pasta for her spaghetti supper.

"Mimi!" Sissy shrieked as she opened the back door. "I'm here!"

"Just in time to help me finish Papaw's supper.

Have you eaten?" Joanne reached down for a big hug from her granddaughter.

"Not yet," Sissy said as she gave her grandmother a giant squeeze.

"Hi, Mom." Melanie greeted Joanne with the usual peck on the cheek. "Here's her suitcase. I'll have the carpool pick her up at your house. Call me if you get too busy and need me to come get her, OK?"

"We'll be fine," Joanne reassured her daughter. "Sylvan and Sara will be over in a minute while Rebecca goes to the hospital to see a friend. Sissy can help watch them."

"Oh, Mom, are you sure?" Melanie placed both hands on her hips for emphasis.

"Like I said, we'll be fine!"

But the evening proved to be more challenging than Joanne had anticipated. It didn't take her long to realize that spaghetti wasn't the best dinner for toddlers, and she wondered if the kids actually got any noodles inside their mouths. After the meal the babies were into everything, and Joanne felt as though she spent the whole time cleaning up messes instead of enjoying her little ones. Sissy proved to be great help, but Joanne hated to keep asking her to entertain her cousins.

Two phone calls from friends at church and a

stopped-up sink didn't help matters, and by the time Rebecca came to pick up the two toddlers and the hastily frosted cake, Joanne was exhausted. She still had to help Sissy go over her spelling words and take a bath. She was thankful that at least her granddaughter's memory was still intact, and they were able to get through the words fairly quickly.

"Sissy, I'll run your bath water while you go get your suitcase," Joanne said, yawning and rubbing her aching back.

"JOANNE . . . telephone." Her husband called out over the sound of running water. "It's your mother."

Joanne knew this would be a long phone call, so she told Sissy to go ahead and bathe herself. Even though, at seven years old, Sissy was fully capable of doing that and washing her own hair, Joanne felt a twinge of guilt at not being able to help her. She reached over and pulled Sissy close to her. "I am so proud of you for being able to take care of yourself and for helping me with your cousins. After your bath, I'll read you a story," she promised.

The phone call took longer than Joanne expected, though, and soon she looked up to see a squeaky clean, wet-headed Sissy sitting beside her. She was already in her pajamas, so Joanne whispered that she needed to go ahead and get in bed and that she would be in soon. Sissy looked disappointed but shuffled off to the bedroom she always slept in.

When Joanne finished the conversation with her mother, she hurried off to check on Sissy. Her heart sank a little when she found Sissy already fast asleep, her angelic face surrounded by wet curls. She gathered up her wet hair so it wouldn't rest on her shoulders, straightened the blanket, and gave her a kiss.

"I'm sorry, sweetheart," she whispered in her granddaughter's ear. "We'll read a book next time."

Too tired to tackle the bookkeeping or the Sunday-school material, Joanne finished putting the dishes in the dishwasher and decided that now was a good time for her to soak in the tub. She turned the dimmer switch down in the bathroom and lit an aroma-therapy candle.

"Boy, do I need this," she said aloud, feeling the warm water graze her fingertips as she brought it to a good bath temperature.

Her large sunken bathtub was used more often as a mini-swimming pool by her grandchildren than as a comfort station for herself, but tonight it was her turn. She was feeling every bit of being a grandmother. Sylvan was a big two-year-old, and every time he came to visit, Joanne ended up feeling like she needed a trip to the chiropractor. She wiped up the sloshed water from Sissy's bath and gathered a clean towel and washcloth for herself.

She stepped into the tub and, with her eyes closed, settled down into the warmth that immediately relaxed her tired body. *Poor Sissy*, she thought. *All she wanted was a little attention.* She remembered her granddaughter's dejected expression. *I wish I could soak that away.* Joanne sighed and opened her eyes.

Through the steam, something red, blue, and yellow caught her attention. *Probably some leftover toys from the kids.* As she leaned forward, there on the side of the tub, just above the water level and written with colored-gel bath soaps, was a message: "I love you, Mimi."

Joanne could barely swallow the lump in her throat as she thought of the little girl lovingly and determinedly finding a way to connect with her grandmother. She smiled as a tear slipped down her cheek. No aroma therapy could match this. However hectic things got, nothing could interrupt the love between a grandmother and her granddaughter.

Understanding the Past

Chapter Two

19

Celebrate your differences. You are My treasured masterpiece. You can be confident that I'll always complete the unique work I've started in you.

Creatively,
Your Forever Faithful God

—from Romans 12:6; Ephesians 2:10; Philippians 1:6

Sometimes it's hard to understand the past—to see how it connects to the present and links inevitably to the future. But it does.

You, granddaughter, are the one who will carry on the traditions established by your grandparents and reinforced by your parents. You're an invaluable link in the family chain. You've heard stories and seen pictures that have the power to bring the stability of the past to the confusion of the present and the uncertainty of the future.

Your family is depending on you to hang on to those traditions. They're part of what identifies you as a family and gives you a distinctive bond. Perhaps you had an Indian grandmother who still

wore a sari on special occasions, or a grandfather who remembered the old Irish songs and sang
them with a thick brogue. Maybe your grandmother
always baked a coconut cake at Easter. Whatever the
traditions, you know the stories behind them. And you
strive to keep the family spirit alive—for yourself, your
children, and eventually your grandchildren.

Few things are more important to our future than
our past—especially how we use the lessons we've
learned to impact the world around us.

Granddaughter, as you preserve the parts
of your past, the memories flavored with
meaning, may they add as much rich-
ness to your life as you add to the
lives of those around you.

*You are here
to enrich the world.
You impoverish
yourself if you forget
this errand.*

Woodrow Wilson

"You look so beautiful," Jennifer's grandmother gushed. But Jennifer wrinkled her nose in disgust.

the art of
being different

"Mom, it just doesn't matter," fourteen-year-old Jennifer Maddox yelled from the top of the staircase, straining to keep her voice within the limits she knew her mother would allow without dealing out punishment.

"It matters to me." Jennifer heard the exasperation in her mother's voice but chose to ignore it. She knew her mother was downstairs gathering up the last-minute items needed for the party, but Jennifer's mind was solely on her clothes.

"But you're the only one who cares! Nana never cares what I wear. Pleeeease!" Her plea seemed to fall on deaf ears. Her mother didn't even acknowledge her words.

Stomping back into her room, Jennifer grabbed the dress her mother had picked out for her and kicked off the army boots she had wanted to wear. "Why did I have to be born into this family," she grumbled to herself. "What a boring mother—she's never any fun!"

Her scowl faded a little as she caught a glimpse of herself in the mirror and paused to admire her reflection. Her new hairstyle with its short, bleached-and-spiked tips was perfect for her small face. She couldn't believe her uptight mother had agreed to let her get such a cool cut. Then she touched her newly pierced left ear. *I can't wait to show Nana*, she thought as she relished her success last Saturday: talking her mom into letting her have not just one but two holes in her left ear. *Now I'm getting somewhere*, she had thought. Today she was a little more cynical. *Mom must have been in a really good mood that day—unlike today, when she insists on my wearing this stupid dress!*

Somewhere in the back of Jennifer's mind, she knew she loved her mother very much. But they were so different. Jennifer's casual, slightly edgy attitude clashed with her mother's more reserved world-view. To say they approached life from different angles was an understatement, and tonight's showdown had been just one more in an endless series over the years.

"Jen, please hurry. Your grandma's party starts at seven, and I'm in charge of greeting the guests."

Jennifer took in a deep breath and rolled her eyes. *She's always in charge of something.* She reached over her head to finish zipping up her dress. *I wish she could just chill out for one day.*

"Time to go," her mom shouted from the end of the staircase. "I'll be in the car."

Jennifer took one more look in the mirror and muttered to herself. "What's so wrong with wanting to wear jeans instead of a dress? She thinks everyone should be just like she is. Doesn't she understand that I'm a person too?"

She spiked her hair a little higher, then stomped out of her bedroom. She made sure the door slammed behind her, knowing there was no one in the house to hear the sound of protest, but still feeling better for having done it.

The drive to her grandma's seventieth birthday party was silent except for the overflow of blaring music she defiantly made sure could be heard from her headset. She didn't want to risk a conversation with her mother. She bobbed her head up and down and back and forth to the beat and, for a moment, lost herself in the music.

"Jennifer, could you please turn the volume down. I can't hear myself think, and I'm not even wearing the earphones! You're going to lose your hearing one day." Jennifer rolled her eyes again and turned the volume down one level.

They arrived at the restaurant before any of the guests, but Jennifer's grandma, Judy, was already sitting in the reception area waiting for them. Jennifer loved her grandmother immensely. They shared a unique bond because they were both artists. Her grandma loved to paint and had introduced Jennifer to the world of color and design at an early age. To her grandmother's delight, Jennifer had taken to art naturally and showed promising talent. Together they had created many masterpieces—most decorating the retired woman's refrigerator but masterpieces just the same.

Jennifer greeted her grandmother with a big hug. "Nana, what do you think of my haircut?"

Judy held Jennifer by the shoulders at arm's length to get a good look. "Why, I think it looks just like you," she answered diplomatically. "You always look beautiful to me. And what's that I see in your ear?"

"Isn't it cool? Mom let me do it last weekend. Everyone's getting their ears pierced multiple times."

Now Jennifer's mother rolled her eyes. "You always say to pick your battles," she said with a resigned smile. "Happy birthday, Mom." She gave her mother a hug.

"Thank you, sweetheart. It's wonderful of you and your brother to do this for me. I hope you didn't go to too much trouble."

"Nonsense! You couldn't turn seventy without a

party. We've been looking forward to this evening. If you'll excuse me for just a minute, I need to check with the manager to make sure everything's ready. Call me picky, but I just can't leave anything to chance. I'll be right back."

"Jennifer, you look so beautiful," Jennifer's grandmother gushed as she motioned for her granddaughter to sit beside her.

Jennifer wrinkled her nose in disgust. "Mom made me wear this dress. I had picked out the coolest black shirt and jeans to wear. And I have a new belt that hangs really low on my hips. But you know Mom, she said I had to look 'nice.' I thought it *did* look nice."

"Yes, I know your mom. I raised her." She chuckled. "And on some days, that was quite a challenge."

"It was?" Jennifer's eyes widened as she waited for the inside scoop on her "perfect" mother.

"You bet. We're just so different. No matter how hard I pushed, she hated art classes. And to be honest, she was never very good—couldn't draw a stick figure. You know, Jennifer, God has given you a gift in your artistic ability. I've seen it from the time you were two years old."

Jennifer could already feel her spirits rise. Her grandmother always had a way of making her feel good about herself.

"Did you and Mom fight about everything?" she

pleaded, wanting more details.

"Well, not everything. You know, it's important to remember that God has made each of us uniquely special. Your mother has many talents I don't have—like organizing and taking charge of things. Sure, I would have liked it if she had been artistic, but what I really wanted was for her to be herself. It's the same with you and your mom—you both have wonderful qualities, they're just different. And that means the things you like to do or the clothes you choose to wear can come into conflict."

"Tell me about it," Jennifer mumbled and hung her head.

Her grandmother lifted Jennifer's face and looked her in the eye. "But Jennifer, don't ever doubt that your mother wants the same for you that I wanted for her—to be your best self. There will be times when you don't agree on things, but those little differences are just about style and individual taste. They have nothing to do with your mother's love for you and her pride in you. Those are unchanging."

Jennifer's shoulders remained slumped. "I know you're probably right, but why doesn't she like anything I like, when you like everything I like?"

Her grandmother smiled sagely. "You have to remember, your mom is the one in the responsible position, while I get to just join in for the fun! When I was raising your mom, I was the one who had to be responsible. That's a much tougher job.

"Speaking of fun . . ." Jennifer's grandmother reached down and pulled a little package from her purse. "I brought you something."

"Nana, I'm the one who's supposed to bring *you* a gift. It's your birthday!" Jennifer laughed with glee at the surprise.

"It's my birthday, and I can give a gift if I want to. After all, it is more fun to give than to receive." She handed Jennifer a tiny box wrapped in pink paper and tied with a black bow.

"I love pink and black! You're the coolest grand-mother ever." Jennifer opened the package and was thrilled to find a new set of pierced earrings—and one extra earring.

"Oh, Nana, they're perfect. I can't wait until I can take out these studs and wear these new earrings. But how did you know I had gotten my ears pierced? I just told you tonight."

Her grandmother smiled and replied with a wink. "Your mother called me and told me how excited you were and how cute you looked. She's really not such a bad mom after all, now is she?"

Jennifer looked down at the earrings and then at

her grandmother. "I guess you're right." Her lips curled up in a smile. "But I'm still glad you're around to be fun with!"

"Me too," her grandmother said. "Now let's go to a party!"

Staying Connected

Chapter Three

Call upon Me and I'll answer you. Find comfort in My ancient ways. My unfailing love is your solace. No matter what, I'm committed to you! I'm always watching over your life.

Loving you always,
Your God of All Comfort

—from Jeremiah 33:3; Psalm 119:52, 76;
Deuteronomy 31:6; Psalm 121:8; 2 Corinthians 1:3

In the hustle and bustle of your day, amid all the exciting challenges in your life, you probably sometimes feel you don't have the time to keep up with family—to make that phone call or write that letter. But you do it anyway, because as a granddaughter you know the importance of staying connected to the people who love you and whom you love.

It's said that no man is an island, and you know that's true. As you navigate through life with its twists and turns, you and your grandparents have been there for each other. Whether it's their cheers at a ball game or their birthday cards with an extra ten dollars in them, your holiday visits or your phone calls just to say hi, you share a special bond

with them because you are a special granddaughter.

Staying connected is easier today than when your
grandparents were children, but it still takes time,
effort, and care. Maybe even more so because we're all
moving so fast it's hard to slow down and take time for
relationships. But when we do, we weave a rich tapes-
try of love. That's a lesson you learned from your
grandparents, and it's a blessing you give back to
them every time you call, write, or e-mail just to
say I love you.

Sure, times have changed. But with
wonderful granddaughters like you,
staying connected remains a time-
less treasure.

If I can put one touch of rosy sunset into the life of any man or woman, I shall feel that I have worked with God.

◆

George MacDonald

Missy put her head in her hands, feeling close to tears. "Working in New York is something I've always wanted to do. Why am I feeling so torn all of a sudden?"

the comfort quilt

Missy meandered through her grandmother's house, acutely aware of her surroundings. Rubbing her fingers along the antique dining-room table, she thought of the many meals she had eaten there. Even now her grandmother was in the kitchen preparing a special dinner for her. The humming she heard over the chopping and dicing was her grandma's favorite hymn. The scent, overpowering even the cinnamon potpourri synonymous with her grandmother's inviting home, was from Missy's favorite dish, roast beef. She stopped for a moment to savor the aroma, her mouth watering in anticipation.

And He walks with me and He talks with me. Silently, Missy filled in the words to the tune coming from the kitchen. *Mamaw has taught me so much,* she thought as she continued her farewell tour through the house. She looked over the dining-room table,

43

past the antique furniture and accents perfectly arranged to break up the long space across the front of the house, to the far side of the living room. *I'll bet I could make it to the couch blindfolded.*

For twenty-four years she had been a part of this house. She had played dominoes and checkers on every tabletop, hide-and-seek in every closet and under every bed. She'd dressed up dolls and pushed them in their miniature strollers from one room to the next. Missy closed her eyes. This was as good a time as any to try her walk of faith. She set off toward the couch. Within seconds she had reached the sofa unhindered and sat down, snuggling a pillow to her chest and breathing in the clean, familiar smell.

Hours on this couch, she thought. Scenes of late-night talks with her grandmother ran through her mind: When she was six, she had asked her grandmother what happens when pets die. As a teenager she had cried to her about awful dates. She'd done countless homework assignments stretched out here. More recently she had announced with excitement— and a little fear—the job offer in New York City. How encouraging and assuring her grandmother had been.

Why am I feeling so torn all of a sudden? Working in New York is something I've always wanted to do. I can't back out now. Missy put her head in her hands, feeling close to tears.

"Missy," her grandmother called out. "Would you set the table for me? I'm running a little behind."

Missy took a deep breath and straightened her back, forcing herself back into composure. "Sure, give me a minute. I'm just checking on a few things."

She stood up and started back toward the dining room but couldn't help pausing when she caught sight of the quilt rack. Her grandmother always had a handmade quilt hanging there, waiting to be given to someone who needed special care. Her family had dubbed them comfort quilts. Growing up, Missy had watched her grandmother quilt her way through every triumph and tragedy. She quilted for the birth of new babies, and she quilted for friends who were hospital bound. Missy couldn't help but walk over and finger the edges. The needlework seemed to represent everything her grandmother stood for: courage, hospitality, resourcefulness, caring. For some reason, tonight the quilt felt almost magical. Missy had never really paid much attention to the pattern or the choice of fabrics. But tonight she noticed. The varying shades of blue had been stitched together masterfully, each shade complementing the others.

Wow, this one is really beautiful. I love blue. I can't believe I never had Mamaw teach me to quilt. She sighed deeply, feeling suddenly remorseful at the lost opportunity, then joined her grandmother in the kitchen.

"What was that?" her grandmother asked.

"Oh, nothing, Mamaw. Everything smells wonderful!" She gave her grandmother a kiss on the cheek. "Thank you for doing this for me. I'm going to miss this so much!"

"It's a labor of love." Her grandmother returned the kiss. "And don't go acting like you won't be back. Any time you're in town, this kitchen will be open for service. Right now we had better hurry. Your parents will be here in fifteen minutes, and we're not quite ready. You know how your daddy hates to wait!"

Missy smiled as she thought of her dad coming in, removing the lid from the roast, and saying, "Smells good, when do we eat?"

"Let's use the good china tonight," her grandmother suggested. "You know where everything is."

Missy went to the dining room and carefully lifted the plates from the china cabinet. Once her grandma had explained how Grampa had surprised her with the china on their fifteenth wedding anniversary. He had shopped and shopped, looking for the perfect pattern to surprise his wife. As Missy peered at her reflection in the cream-colored plates with their gold rims, she thought her grandpa had done a great job. *It must not look a day older than it did when Grandma opened the original box.* She raised an eyebrow. *Of course, it's not like it should be worn out from overuse. I'll bet I could count on my fingers how many times I've seen these plates out. Special occasions, that's it.* Suddenly it sunk in that this time *she* was the special occasion.

"Oh, Missy," her grandma called from the kitchen. "Can you also set out the silverware? A few spoons are missing, but there should be enough."

Missy grinned. She knew the missing spoons were probably her doing back when she was a child holding pretend tea parties.

Just then she heard the front door open and a loud "Mmm-mm. Something sure smells good! When do we eat?"

Missy shook her head and laughed. *There's Dad.*

"How about a hug and then I'll think about putting food on the table?" she heard her grandma say. "First things first!"

"That's what I was talking about. First things first. Where's the food?"

Missy hung back, listening to the familiar banter. *That, I will miss. It's hard to capture that in a letter or an e-mail.*

"Hey, Mom and Dad." Missy went to the kitchen and hugged each of her parents.

"What do I need to do?" her mom asked as she washed her hands, preparing to help.

Missy's grandmother directed her answer at her son, who was picking at the roast with a fork. "We're just waiting on the rolls."

"All right, all right. Can I help it if I think you're a fabulous cook? Do you want me to carve the roast?"

"Yes, if you think you can keep from eating the whole thing in the process!"

Soon the roast was on the table, the rolls were buttered, and the family was seated and talking animatedly about the adventures of their week. Missy soaked in every detail, relishing the laughter and love that filled the room. Finally, she cleared her throat. "Can I have your attention please?" She swallowed hard, not wanting to cry just yet.

"I know I'm not leaving for a few days, but I've been thinking about what it means to be part of a family that loves and supports you. And I've concluded it means everything. Tonight I got here early because I wanted some quiet time alone in this house, touching, smelling, and remembering everything I've done here.

"There's something extraordinary about a grandparent's house that I can't quite explain. It's like your own house because you feel like everything is yours, yet you're treated like a special guest. I want to thank you, Mamaw, for the heritage of a family whose greatest tradition is to love one another. It all started with you and Grandpa. You two passed it on to Daddy, and he and Mom have taught me. I just want you all to know that no matter where I am, you are the most important people in the world to me, and I love you."

Missy's mother picked up a napkin and dabbed away a tear. Her dad pretended to be clearing his throat. Missy's grandmother was the first to speak, her voice thick with emotion. "Well, if I can manage it, I have something special to share too." The room got even quieter as she got up and walked over to stand behind Missy.

Missy closed her eyes, sure she couldn't hold back tears much longer.

"You all know how much I love this little girl." Her grandmother patted Missy on the shoulder as if she were still five years old. "I know she's all grown up, but she's still my little Missy. Her decision to move to New York is a brave one, and I want her to know how proud I am of her adventurous spirit and her desire to make her own way. But she's right— family is the most precious gift we have. So I have something for you—for the days when you're missing that family connection and you need someone to wrap loving arms around you and hold you tight." She made her way over to the quilt rack.

Missy held her breath as her grandmother picked up the quilt and began unfolding it with as much care and ceremony as a marine unfolding the American flag. As she exposed each layer, the hours of work it had obviously taken, the tiny stitches that formed an intricate design, were evidence of how she loved Missy.

Missy rose and wrapped her arms around her grandmother, quilt and all. "Oh, Mamaw, this is for me? It's the best gift ever!"

"Wait," her grandmother said with a gleam in her eye. "You haven't seen the best part."

Missy helped her grandmother unfold the quilt the rest of the way. When it was open, her grandmother instructed her to turn it over and look at the other side.

Missy gasped. She couldn't believe her eyes. Right in the middle of the quilt was a collage of pictures that had been scanned onto the individual squares of fabric—Missy and her parents and grandparents at various stages of their lives. Now the tears were unstoppable, and Missy grabbed her grandmother again in a tight embrace. Their special bond had been captured forever in the most beautiful quilt she had ever seen. Now, no matter where she was, all she had to do to feel at home was touch the comfort quilt.

Feeling
Loved

Chapter Four

You can't begin to measure My love for you. It's even better than life. I keep My covenant of love to a thousand generations. You can count on My goodness and love every day.

Eternal hugs,
Your God of Love

—from Psalms 103:11; 63:3; Deuteronomy 7:9; Psalm 23:6

Isn't it fun to be the center of attention? Whether it's your kindergarten graduation or your wedding day, you are *it*! All the cameras and lights are on you.

But special occasions only come along once in a while. Want to enjoy that special place of importance every day? You don't have to climb Mount Everest or win a beauty contest. You don't have to prove or earn anything. You are a granddaughter.

The moment you came into this world, you changed your grandparents' lives forever— just by being you. You give them someone to love, someone to shower attention on and to delight in. And the best thing is it doesn't have to be a

inspirational message

special day, like a graduation or a wedding, for you to be the most important person in the world to them. It can just be any day and anytime—it's every day and all the time.

You are reason enough for celebration—no special occasion needed. It doesn't matter what you look like or how talented you are or what anyone else thinks of you. Your grandparents think you're perfect just the way you are. Their hearts were given to you on an unconditional silver platter the minute you were born. No matter what else happens, you, granddaughter, hold an irrevocable place of importance in their hearts.

The measure of
God's love
is that He loves
without measure.

St. Bernard

Everything was in place
for the wedding
of her dreams.
There had been no
snags . . . until now.

in sickness and in health

Shelly looked at her fresh set of French-manicure sculpted nails. *If they weren't so lovely, I'd bite them right off.* She was so nervous that her old nail-biting habit had returned with a vengeance. But her grandmother had treated her and her bridesmaids to manicures the day before, and now as she placed her hands delicately on the white skirt of her wedding gown, her thoughts again returned to her grandma.

This can't be happening. She sighed and started pacing the floor of the tiny bride's room.

There had been no snags until now. The flowers were the exact color she wanted. The bridesmaids' dresses fit perfectly. The rehearsal had gone smoothly. Everything was in place for the wedding of her dreams, and she knew the credit went to her grandmother, who had poured countless hours of love and energy into making this day as wonderful as even a princess could have wished.

Shelly's grandmother had been a much sought-after wedding planner. Mothers had loved her attention to detail, and fathers her ability to work magic with any wedding budget. When she retired ten years earlier, she had promised Shelly she would come out of retirement to plan her only granddaughter's wedding. Since Shelly was a girl, they had poured over bride magazines together, picking out the perfect flowers and designing and redesigning wedding cakes—all in anticipation of the day Shelly would walk down the aisle in a fairy-tale setting created by her grandmother.

But just a few hours ago, Shelly's mother had tapped her gently on the shoulder. "Shelly, I don't want you to panic. Everything is OK. I just have to tell you something."

Speechless, Shelly had just stared at her mother. Surely those words on your wedding day would seem the perfect time to panic. The possibilities were swirling in her imagination: the cake falling on its way to the church, the church catching fire from a stray candle, the photographer not showing up . . .

"Don't panic!" She remembered her voice catching somewhere in her throat before squeaking out. "What does that mean? What happened?" She had tried to stay calm, but a sickening feeling had taken hold of her stomach almost instantly.

"Your grandpa just called, and Grandma is at the hospital. She wasn't feeling well when she woke up this morning, but she just kept going to make sure everything was ready for tonight."

Shelly's eyes widened as she listened to the details, now focused on her grandmother's health and not yet considering the impact the news would have on her own plans. Her mother continued. "She was talking to the florist one last time when nausea overcame her, and she became very sick."

"She'll be OK by the wedding, won't she?" The expression in her voice was seeking confirmation rather than an answer to a question.

"Well, honey," Shelly's mom responded guardedly, "Grandpa said he took her on to the hospital hoping they could give her something to get her through the wedding, but he said he wasn't sure it would work."

Somewhere in the middle of her concern for her grandmother's health, it hit her. The candles were only minutes away from being lit, the finishing touches of pink roses were being added to the three-tier cake— and her wedding planner was in the hospital.

"Oh, Mom." Shelly bit her lip. "She's the one who knows everything. When the music starts, who wears a corsage, when the candle lighters start—"

"We'll be just fine," Shelly's mom said reassuringly. "We practiced last night, and everyone knows what to do. Besides, I've heard your grandmother say many times, 'You can't mess up a wedding.'"

Shelly could hear her grandmother's voice in those words, and she relaxed a little, but she still didn't like the thought of her strong, always proper grandma on a gurney in the emergency room. The matriarch of their family stood five feet, ten inches tall, with piercing blue eyes and Clairol-brown hair. No one ever suspected she was seventy-five years old. She was a tower of strength to Shelly—someone she called whenever she needed sound, no-nonsense advice.

"Mom, remember last night when Grandma insisted on bringing a fruit tray to have here for the bridesmaids to munch on? I'll bet she's thinking about that right now. She wanted everything to be so perfect."

"I'm sure you're right." Her mom shook her head and smiled. "She's probably still trying to figure out how she can get a fruit tray up here. Grandpa said to tell you she whispered between waves of nausea, 'Tell Shelly not to worry. At six o' clock, I'll be there!'"

Shelly's lip quivered as she thought of her sweet grandmother, with whom she had shared so many of her wedding dreams, not being able to see it all come true. She closed her eyes and said a prayer for her grandmother's health.

"Mom, should we postpone the wedding for an hour or so? Grandma would be so sad if she missed it. What should we do?"

"Sweetie, it's too late to change the schedule now. The music will start at six o'clock, and you will walk down the aisle just as you and your grandmother planned." Shelly's mom reached over and grabbed her worried daughter's hand. "She had everything organized; the wedding will go smoothly and be lovely. Your grandmother will be sad if she misses it, but she would be beside herself if she knew you were even thinking of delaying it because of her. Grandpa said she'll be fine and for us to not worry. Now let's get downstairs for pictures."

Shelly hoped and prayed that her smile didn't look too fixed in the photo session as she tried to remain calm and not focus too much on her grandma's illness. She had made her mother promise to keep her updated if any news came in.

The last call her mother received was at four o'clock, and Shelly's grandmother was being released but was still very sick. "Dad, tell her to go straight home and rest. The wedding will be videotaped, and she can watch it later."

Shelly was listening to her mother talk and

wanted to agree with her, yet she couldn't help wishing her grandmother would come to the wedding. After all the years of planning, it was almost unthinkable to go through it without her.

Shelly looked at her watch. Five-fifteen. *She's not going to make it. How can I get married without Grandma?*

Just then the door opened and her mother appeared. "They want us to start lining up. Are you ready?"

Shelly knew her mom was doing her best to be cheerful and positive and to ensure that her special day wasn't ruined.

"Sure, Mom," Shelly said, blinking back a tear.

"Let me have one last hug before I have to share you forever with the man of your dreams." Her mom held her extra tight as she whispered, "Here's a hug from your grandmother. She'll love the pictures. You look beautiful!"

"Thank you, Momma." Shelly sniffled and took a deep breath. "I'm ready. I guess that old saying is true: 'The best laid plans of mice and men often go awry.' I sure didn't expect Grandma to miss this wedding, but I know it'll be OK."

"That's my girl! You know, your grandmother would say wild horses couldn't keep her from being at your wedding. You know she'd be here if she could."

Shelly's mom walked behind her to hold the long, beaded train in the air as Shelly walked down the hall and into the foyer of the church building. Shelly clung to her flowers and nervously played with her engagement ring as she practiced the timing of her steps, mentally humming the wedding march.

Her dad greeted her at the back of the chapel. "Where did my little girl go?" he asked as he kissed her cheek. "I haven't seen such a beautiful bride since your mother took my breath away twenty-five years ago." Seeing her stoic father tear up surprised her and tore at her heart.

"Oh, Daddy—" She returned her dad's kiss and smiled as she wiped the faint lipstick smudge off his cheek. "I love you so much."

The bridesmaids were taking their slow walk toward the stained-glass front of the chapel. Shelly could see that the little sanctuary was almost full with her family and friends. Everything was perfect. *Grandma would have loved this.*

Suddenly the music changed, and she felt her father's nudge to move up to the archway where their walk would begin. She caught her breath as she saw everyone stand and face her. This was it—the moment she had dreamed of.

Shelly smiled as her dad patted her arm. She felt almost as if she were gliding down the aisle on a magic carpet, her gaze meeting that of her husband-to-be. Then, as if by impulse, she looked toward the pew where her grandparents were to be seated—and discovered, to her surprise, that they were right where they were supposed to be, smiling and crying!

She couldn't make herself keep walking. She had to stop and hug her grandma. "Grandma, what are you doing? I thought you were going home after they released you!"

"I promised you I'd be here at six o'clock. Wild horses couldn't have kept me from sharing this day with you!"

Shelly laughed and took her place again beside her dad. As she started back down the aisle, she mouthed "I love you" to her grandmother. She didn't have to wait for her grandmother to mouth it back. She already knew.

Being Supportive

Chapter Five

Even before you ask, I know your needs. I am able to provide all of your needs according to My unlimited riches in glory. You can wait in hope for Me because I'm your help and your protection.

Supporting you,
Your Heavenly Father

—from Matthew 6:8; Philippians 4:19; Psalm 33:20

Only a handful of people know almost everything about you. It's a small minority that knows whether you eat spinach or like scary movies. Your parents, maybe your best friend . . . and your grandparents. Having people around who know you so well that they can sense a need and act on it is one of the best feelings in the world, and that's just the kind of feeling a grandparent-granddaughter relationship can bring.

Yet you've never allowed yourself to stay only on the receiving end of your grandparents' affection. You give your amazing love and support to them as well. And through the years, they've come to know they can depend on you. Your love for them and your concern for their well-being is evident and invaluable. While they would do anything for you, what's even more special is knowing you would do anything for them.

That's what a support system is. It sustains you through good times and bad. Whether it's late at night or early in the morning, you're there for each other.

Today's society is mobile, and grandparents may be more active for longer than ever before—traveling, taking classes, or launching second careers. But they still need you and want to be part of your life. A loving, supportive relationship with you, their granddaughter, is a joy and a blessing.

The smallest seed
of faith is better than
the largest fruit
of happiness.

◆

Henry David Thoreau

Anne chased her giggling, diaper-trailing toddler down the hall. "What am I doing wrong?" she lamented.

the dinner guest

Anne was up to her ears in poop. Well, almost. She had a baby in diapers, a toddler being potty trained, and two cats that had suddenly developed an aversion to their litter pan. Sometimes she felt as though her entire day revolved around cleaning something up.

Today had been no different, and she was exhausted. But finally, for a few precious minutes, the house was relatively quiet. Two-year-old Jesse was entertaining himself in his room; baby Gracie was sitting quietly on Anne's lap, and the cats had been put out to wander in the yard. Anne wouldn't have been too disappointed if they wandered away entirely.

She had just picked up a novel she was determined to read when the phone rang. Anne sighed. She was tired of all the telemarketing calls and was sorely tempted to ignore it—to launch her own personal phone strike. But she put the book down, hiked Gracie on one hip, and picked up the receiver. *Maybe it's Calgon calling to take me away*, she thought wryly.

"Hi, Anne, this is Granny. How are you?"

"Oh, Granny. Hi! I'm fine. How are you?" It was almost as good as Calgon. Anne loved the sound of her grandmother's voice. It was so soothing and always sincere.

"Well, honey, I'm doing pretty well. I just wanted to see how my babies were."

"They're great too. But Granny, I think I started this whole process too late. You had your babies young, when you had lots of energy. I thought after running an office, motherhood would be easy. I had no idea how hard this could be."

Granny Grace laughed. "I seem to recall someone who said having babies in her thirties would mean she'd be more mature and able to handle it." Even when she was teasing, Anne could hear the sympathy in her grandmother's voice.

"Did I say that? What was I thinking?" Anne laughed too, knowing it was the truth. "Although I seem to recall someone saying, 'You're probably right!'"

Granny Grace sighed in happy resignation. "You know I'll support you, whatever you say."

"I know. Really, the kids are great. Jesse's ear infection cleared up, and Gracie is growing like a little weed."

Just then Jesse came running through the house with his diaper in hand and its contents spilling on the floor.

"What am I doing wrong?" she lamented into the phone. "Here comes Jesse with his diaper off, leaving a trail for me to clean up. I guess I'd better go. I love you. We'll talk soon. Maybe we can go to lunch later this week."

Anne barely heard her grandmother's reply as she hung up the phone and went after Jesse. "Stop, right this minute," she yelled as she chased a giggling Jesse down the hall. *Why didn't I ask Granny how she potty trained nine kids and lived to tell about it?*

Catching her energetic toddler with one hand while clinging to the baby with the other hand wasn't an easy task. Now she had to figure out how to get everyone clean and supper on the table by six o'clock. Her husband, Jack, had been out of town on business, and she'd promised him a home-cooked meal on his return. She wanted to tell him it would be much easier if he brought home pizza, but he never quite understood how busy her days were. Those few lines she got to read in her novel constituted the only break she'd had the entire day.

Being Supportive

Looking at her watch, she realized it was already four thirty and time was running out. *What do I have in the freezer*, she thought as she scrubbed the wood floor for the third time that day. *Maybe the ham is still in there from Christmas. I could thaw it in the microwave . . .*

The phone rang again. Anne got up from her knees and made her way into the kitchen once again. *I'm too old for this.*

"Hello," she answered, trying to sound more pleasant than she felt.

"Hi, honey! How's your day going? It's really been busy at the office. I got back in around noon, and you know how hard it is to play catch-up."

Anne stood with a Lysol can in one hand and a mop in the other as she listened to her husband's cheerful voice. "Same here," she managed to say. "Just as busy as little bees!"

"Great," Jack chirped. "I can't wait to see you guys. I hope you don't mind, but since you were cooking tonight anyway, I asked Donnie from accounting to come for dinner. We've been trying to get together on that project for a week now, and I figured tonight's as good a night as any."

Anne's silence spoke volumes, but Jack didn't notice. "Are you still there? Can you hear me?"

"I'm here. What time did you want to eat?" Anne's voice was as frosty as an old freezer.

"I was thinking we would come a little early so we don't have to work too late," Jack replied, seemingly oblivious to his wife's dilemma. "How about five-thirty? He's single, so don't worry too much about the house. He'll just be happy for a home-cooked meal."

"Great, see you soon." Anne put the phone rather firmly in its cradle and added sarcastically, "Oh, you mean he won't mind a little mess on the floor as long as I have some good food?"

She finished cleaning the hallway and went to the laundry room to put away her cleaning supplies. *I will remain calm . . . I will remain calm . . .* she began chanting in her head.

The sound of splashing water caught her attention, and she bolted into the bathroom to find Gracie tottering over the toilet, the water just within her reach, having the time of her life.

"Oh, Gracie, no, no. The potty isn't a toy." But Gracie didn't agree and managed one more splash before Anne whisked her away.

Anne sat Gracie on the bathroom counter and lathered her down with soap. Gracie dangled her little feet in the sink, finding another new game to play.

As she watched her daughter in the mirror, Anne couldn't resist smiling at the chubby little face and beautiful brown eyes looking back at her. Her hair was soaked and formed one little curl on her forehead.

"OK, you are adorable, but your daddy is expecting dinner in forty-five minutes, and I haven't even started!"

"Come on, you little monkey. Let's get some clean clothes on you, and then I have to think about supper."

Anne smoothed baby lotion on Gracie, put pajamas on her, and placed her in the highchair with a handful of Cheerios on the tray. "There, now you'll stay out of trouble for a while. I'm not so sure about your brother."

She headed back down the hall to check on Jesse, but before she reached his bedroom, the doorbell rang. Anne sighed, rolling her eyes in despair. "What now?" She peeked in Jesse's room, not wanting him to see her, and was thrilled to see that he was still quietly playing. She tip-toed backward and then headed for the front door. "If this is a vacuum-cleaner salesman, I will not be responsible for my actions," she warned no one in particular.

"Granny, what are you doing here?" Anne exclaimed, surprised at this unexpected visit. "Come in!"

"We didn't get to finish our conversation earlier, so I decided to come on over anyway." Anne's mouth dropped opened as she watched her grandmother waltz past with her hands full of potholders and saucepans. "I fixed your family some dinner. I called to tell you, but those babies were keeping you too busy to listen. Anyway, when your grandpa was alive, he used to say, 'Don't ask if you can help, just go ahead and do it.' So here I am. I hope you don't mind. If you've already made something, you can just save this for tomorrow. There's nothing here that won't keep."

Anne was speechless. *How could she know?* Her eyes welled up with tears of relief and gratitude as she hugged her grandmother. "Granny, you will never know how much I needed this tonight," she whispered.

"Oh, I think I already do. I'm not too old to remember—been there, done that!"

They shared a good laugh and, arm in arm, headed to the car to unload the rest of the dinner.

Facing
the Unknown

Chapter Six

When you face the unknown, seek Me and I'll answer you, delivering you from all your fears. When you look to Me, you'll shine. Come to me with all of your worries, because I care deeply for you. Find the secret of being joyful in hope, patient in trouble, and faithful in prayer.

Guiding you,
Your God of Hope

—from Psalm 34:4–5; 1 Peter 5:7; Romans 12:12

Contemplating the future can be fun, but sometimes it can also be frightening. Years ago explorers made their way over treacherous mountains or through dangerous woodlands to secure their future family homes. They were willing to risk their very lives to guarantee a better future for their children and grandchildren.

Times have changed, and we rarely have to risk our lives to make sure of our future. Still, the uncertainty of where our future might take us can be scary. Generations have gone before you, but you'll need to make your own mark on the world. You probably won't be called on to forge your way through the wilderness, but you still must navigate the rough terrain of choices that will determine the course of your life.

Daunting, isn't it? You may wonder if you're ready to forge ahead into the unknown.

You are.

You've watched those who have gone before you. Their experience has been your training. It's never easy to accept responsibility, to realize that others are now looking to you as the pioneer who will clear a path for them. But Granddaughter, face the future with confidence, knowing that you are loved. That you will always be in our hearts. That whatever life demands, you can do it.

Every experience
God gives us,
every person He puts
in our lives, is the
perfect preparation
for the future
that only He can see.

♦

Corrie ten Boom

The left turn into the
driveway nearly took
her breath away
as she realized how
unprepared she was
for this moment.

love remembers

The short one-hour trip from Alexandria to Natchitoches, Louisiana, felt instead like a tedious cross-country journey. Kaitlyn's eyelids were leaden from lack of sleep, but her heart was even heavier. She blinked hard to try to bring some moisture back into her tired eyes and struggled to think of something besides Grandma and Grandpa Jones.

It was no use. She couldn't help reliving the many trips she had taken to that house. She thought of the big family van, coloring books, markers, sticker activities, and tiny cars strewn about on the floor. Her mom had tried everything to keep sibling squabbles to a minimum. Eagerly anticipating a week or weekend of Grandma's good cooking and Grandpa's fishing trips, Kaitlyn and her brothers could hardly contain their energy and excitement.

Even now she could almost smell bacon frying and Grandma's homemade biscuits fresh and hot. "You can just pick them up with your fingers and sop them in the syrup," her grandma would tell them. Kaitlyn's mouth watered involuntarily at the most delicious memory of all, the wonderful scent of fresh pecan pie wafting from the oven. She sighed, weighed down with the knowledge that she would never experience days like that again.

She looked right and left to cross an intersection and became conscious of how much the landscape had changed in the thirty years she'd been traveling this small, two-lane highway. The trees were bigger, the gas stations more frequent, and the traffic heavier. *Everything changes*.

Her parents had gone to the house the day before, but Kaitlyn couldn't get off work until the weekend. Her brothers would come when they could get free from jobs and other obligations. But as the oldest grandchild and the only girl, Kaitlyn always felt more responsible to help out.

She turned on the radio to the local Christian station, looking for some comfort. A remix of "I Come to the Garden Alone" was playing, and soon Kaitlyn's eyes were full of tears as she thought of her grandmother's sweet voice singing with the other fifty or so church members on Sundays. No megachurch for her grandmother. "I don't need a lot of folks around me to know I'm doing the right thing," her grandma had told her once. "I just need me and the Lord to worship." Kaitlyn smiled. Her grandmother's dedicated faith had influenced their whole family.

A pothole jarred her to attention, and she realized she was almost to the water tower. "I see it." "I saw it first!" "You didn't call it!" She could hear echoes of the van full of kids arguing about who saw the tower first. They all knew it meant they were just minutes away from Grandma's house.

Natchitoches was the oldest city in the Louisiana Purchase. One downtown street was still made of the original bricks. The Cane River meandered right down the center of the sleepy little town. Kaitlyn's brothers would line up on the riverbank, fishing with Grandpa, while she and her grandmother wiled away the hours browsing in antique stores and eating ice cream. Most of their evenings were spent the same way each trip, frying the fish the boys had caught and laughing about how many hooks Grandpa had to get out of a tree or a floating limb.

Kaitlyn turned right automatically and admired the row of pecan trees that always welcomed her to Grandma's house. *No wonder she baked so many pecan pies.* She breathed in deeply, pretending to get a whiff of a pie cooling on the kitchen counter.

She slowed down as if to take in every sight and sound Watson Lane held that day. *It's the end of an era.* Three children were playing basketball, and two more were riding bikes. A young man was loading up his boat with an ice chest and fishing gear. A young mother was pushing a toddler in a fancy stroller with cup holders, and an older woman walked briskly down the street with her back to Kaitlyn.

Grandma's neighbors . . . I wonder if they know. Some of them probably do. Others may be surprised when the For Sale sign goes up.

The left turn into the driveway nearly took her breath away. She suddenly realized how unprepared she was for this moment. Her grandmother's house without her grandmother. It just didn't seem right.

Even though Grandma had been sick for five years, Grandpa had always taken care of her. Now the disease had progressed, and he was tired. He had called Kaitlyn's mother and said he was ready to move in with her and to put Grandma in a nursing home. It would be better, they all agreed. None of the family lived in Natchitoches, and it was hard for Kaitlyn's mom to check on her elderly parents. With the move back to Alexandria, they would all be able to see each other more often. Today was moving day.

Kaitlyn put the car in park, closed her eyes, and said a prayer for her family as they bid farewell to a house and a life they loved. She walked to the front door, trying to avoid stepping on the pecans that dotted her path. She glanced toward the carport, half expecting the fish fryer to be sending up steam. It wasn't.

The screen door squeaked and squawked as she opened it.

"Well, there you are, honey," her grandpa said from his favorite chair.

Kaitlyn smiled at him, always amazed at how he had stayed the same sweet man in spite of the difficult years of caring for a wife with Alzheimer's. "Hi, Grandpa. How's Grandma doing?"

"She's about the same. She's in her bed." He grew a little somber. "Kaity, she may not recognize you this time, but remember she loves you just the same."

"I know, Gramps. I'll never forget that." Kaitlyn swallowed the lump in her throat and hugged him tightly. "I can't wait to see her. Where's Mom and Dad?"

"Packing up the bedroom. Your mother sent me out here to take a break."

Kaitlyn wished the hallway could be as long as it had seemed when she was younger, but instead it felt shorter than ever. In just a few steps she could see her grandmother staring out the window.

"Hi, Grandma!" She tried to sound cheerful. Her grandmother turned her head as if she was ready to acknowledge the person speaking, but no words came. Kaitlyn sat on the bed beside her.

"Grandma, it's Kaity." She took her grandmother's hand and started the one-sided conversation. "I just got here. It was a beautiful drive over this morning." Searching for words, she added, "Are you looking at those nice pecan trees in the yard?" Kaitlyn watched as her grandma tried unsuccessfully to fit the pieces together. Finally, with a wrinkled brow and a faraway look, her grandmother managed a weak "Hello." It was all Kaitlyn could do to not break down and cry.

"Kaitlyn," her mother called from the guest bedroom. "Come on in here. We have so much to show you."

Kaitlyn kissed her grandma on the forehead and said she'd be right back. She crossed the hall and found her mom and dad knee-deep in memorabilia. School pictures, coloring pages from Sunday-school lessons, old letters, and an assortment of homemade crafts covered the bed and much of the floor.

"Hey, Mom and Dad," Kaitlyn said as she hugged both her parents. "Mom, it's too hard. How are you getting through this?" She picked up a photo of herself and Grandma with their Easter bonnets on. She just stared at the photo, unable to speak further.

"Kaitlyn, it is hard. You're right. We're so caught up in the memories, we can hardly pack. But we're making a little progress. I wanted you to see these things in case we don't unpack them for a while. Someone else in our family needs to know what treasures will be stored in these plastic bins." Kaitlyn was impressed at how neatly her mom was preserving the family mementos.

Her grandfather joined them and surveyed the room with a sweet but heavy sigh. "Kaity, your grandmother loved you kids so much. Just look around this room and you'll see that she always wanted you near her. If she couldn't be at a school play or ball game, she'd have your mother save some item for her so she could feel as though she'd been there. When she got to go, she always brought something back to remind her of the good time she had.

"But she also left something for you. A few years ago, before her memory got too bad, she wrote each of you kids a letter. I've saved them until now. Your grandma knew this time would come, but she was prepared." He handed a letter to Kaitlyn.

Her hands shook as she opened it, and she had to wipe tears from her eyes in order to make out the writing.

Dear Kaity,

I remember standing outside the hospital nursery, watching you wiggle your mouth to form that same dimple your mother has. I think your grandpa had to pry me away after an hour of just staring at you. From that first moment on, I have never been disappointed in you. You have brought nothing but joy to my life.

I know you're sad that I'm not with you as I used to be. But dearest Kaity, while I may be silent on the outside, inside I'm full of memories of you. Look in every drawer and every closet of this house and you'll see evidence of the memories I've tucked away.

I know you're there taking care of me and your grandpa, and I want to thank you for loving us and allowing us to share your life. One more thing—look in the kitchen drawer beside the telephone and get that recipe for pecan pie. I know you can make them just as good as mine!

I love you forever,
Grandma

Tears spilled down Kaitlyn's cheeks as she dissolved into her mother's comforting embrace. Soon they were all holding on to each other in the tiny bedroom on Watson Lane.

"Well," Grandpa said, clearing his throat. "I'm hungry."

Kaitlyn looked down at the letter she still held. "Grandpa, let's go find that recipe. What this house needs is the smell of a fresh pecan pie."

Continuing the Legacy

Chapter Seven

Let My love compel you. Living a legacy of love is the excellent way! Share with others what they need. Let My statutes be your heritage and the joy of your heart. As you live every day, set your heart on following My instructions.

Blessing you,
Your Creator

—from 2 Corinthians 5:14; 1 Corinthians 13:13; Romans 12:13; Psalm 119:111–112

You sit beside them on a riverbank, sharing a fishing pole. You stand on a stool beside them, patting down biscuit dough. You lounge on the back porch with them as you watch frogs play on a hot summer day. You think you're just having a fun day. But what you don't realize is how much joy you're bringing to some of the people who love you most—your grandparents.

Watching a granddaughter laugh and play is one of a grandparent's favorite pastimes. But sharing with her the many valuable lessons we've gained throughout our lives ranks among the most rewarding activities too. Some people say God gave us grandchildren so we could make up for everything we forgot to teach our own children. But that's not really true. It's just that we love you so much we want to do everything we can to equip, inspire, and encourage you to thrive, to make a difference, to leave a legacy.

So thank you for your patience when we seem determined to teach you everything we know. Thanks for spending time with us and for letting us share our hearts with you. For being our best legacy. We couldn't be more proud.

One thing, and only one, in this world has eternity stamped upon it. Feelings pass; opinions change. What you have done lasts— lasts in you. Through ages, through eternity, what you have done for Christ, that, and only that, you are.

F. W. Robertson

"It smells funny. Why do I have to go?" Alicia had pleaded as a child. Now she was glad she'd gone.

cookie day

The smell of freshly baked cookies filled the kitchen as Alicia looked under the table for her daughter's missing shoe. "Come on, sweetie," she yelled from an upside-down position, grabbing the missing shoe with one hand and balancing herself with the other. "The cookies are almost ready. You know how Granny looks forward to this day and will be waiting for us."

She looked up just as five-year-old Amy came running into the kitchen with an armload of dolls. "Mommy, can I take my new Barbies to show Granny? She might want to play with them." The energetic youngster, one shoe on and one shoe off, was peeking through blond and brunette Barbie dolls—two dressed in fancy gowns and two more in the latest sports clothes.

"Sure. Granny will love to see your dolls. Let's get your shoe on, then you can put your dolls in your backpack." Alicia reached down to pick up Amy and set her on the kitchen table, at a more adult-friendly shoe-tying height. "I'll put the cookies in a plastic box. Then we'll be ready to go."

Amy jumped down and ran to the back of the house, pigtails bouncing. Alicia smiled as she thought of how much joy Amy had brought to Granny.

Her grandmother had only been in the nursing home for three months. She was adjusting well, but Alicia knew how important the visits from family and friends were to her. It was her grandmother who had taught her the Biblical principle of caring for those who are "shut in."

It's still hard to believe these trips are now to visit my grandmother instead of going with her to visit others, Alicia thought as she scooped cookies into a plastic container. She shook her head in lingering disbelief. *The same nursing home where she's spent years ministering to the occupants . . . I should be picking her up to go with me, not going to see her there.*

Alicia had only been two years old when her grandmother started including her in her shut-in ministry. Once a week they would bake cookies and head to the nursing home to encourage the patients who lived there. It was clear to Alicia even then that the senior citizens loved seeing someone young, and for many years she loved being the center of attention. But as she got older, Alicia had found the trips less pleasant and had begged her mother to let her stay home.

"Mom, it smells funny. Why do I have to go?" she would plead. *So much complaining about doing such a simple act of kindness*, she thought now.

"Honey, it's so important to your grandmother," her mom had answered. "You'll be glad once you go." That hadn't always been true then, but now she was glad she had gone. She cherished the heritage of love her grandmother had handed down to her and was grateful for the opportunity to hand that down to her own daughter.

"Mommy, I'm ready." Amy pulled at Alicia's jeans, trying to get her attention.

Alicia patted her on the head. "I am too. Let's go."

Once they were on their way, Amy began her usual chattering and asking questions. "Mommy, why does Granny live with all those other people?"

"Remember, I told you Granny is a little sick now, and your Grandma Parker can't take care of her anymore. She needs a nurse to take care of her." Alicia thought of her mother's struggle as she had made the difficult decision to put her own mother in a nursing home.

"Oh, I forgot." Amy seemed satisfied with that simple explanation. Alicia looked in the rearview mirror to see her daughter's contented face. She glanced up at herself in the mirror and noticed that she didn't look quite as peaceful. But she knew the truth—that her grandmother was sicker than "a little." Her chronic lung disease had progressed so that she suffered from frequent bouts of pneumonia. It was a condition she had lived with for years, but at eighty-eight years old, her body was tiring of the fight.

"Mommy, tell me about when you were little and would go to the nursing home with Granny." Amy had asked to hear the familiar story over and over again.

"OK, but you've heard this story so many times. Aren't you tired of it?"

"Nope," Amy responded from the backseat.

"Well, when I was little, every Tuesday morning at 9:45, Granny would pick me up to go to the nursing home with her. She always brought homemade cookies, carefully stacked in a shoe box, for me to pass out to her friends. I would hold the box on my lap as we drove and try to not eat them all before we got there." Alicia let out a little giggle at the memory. "Of course, I couldn't resist at least one. And Granny would make sure she had enough so I could eat one on the way. It was always the same kind of cookie—a tea cake. She said her friends didn't need a lot of sugar, and those didn't have much sugar in them."

"Did they like that kind?"

"You bet. It's the same kind we make when we have time—like we did this morning." Alicia picked up the story again. "In those days, kids didn't have to sit in car safety seats, so I sat right next to Granny. If she had to stop quickly, she'd reach over really fast and hold me back with her arm." She added softly, almost to herself, "I always felt safe with Granny."

Alicia smiled and could almost feel the comfort of snuggling next to her grandmother. "We would sing all the way to the nursing home. 'Jesus Loves Me' and 'Victory in Jesus' were our favorites. Once we got there, Granny would open the door and waltz in like she was famous, and her friends would be waiting for her. Some were in wheelchairs, some were in beds in their rooms, some would be watching TV on the couches. But they all knew who she was and were happy to see her."

"Just like when we go. Right, Mommy?"

Alicia looked again in the mirror to see her daughter grinning. "Just like when we go," she affirmed with a smile. "You know, it makes Granny very happy that we're continuing what she started."

Amy didn't respond, and Alicia glanced back to see a concerned look on her daughter's face.

"Mommy, who will do this when I go to kindergarten?" School would be starting in two weeks.

"You know, I've been thinking about that. When I

was little, Granny went every Tuesday morning—I only went with her in the summer. But since Granny is there now, maybe we could change our cookie day to Tuesday afternoon, after school. How does that sound?"

"I like that idea," Amy responded. "I don't want to stop seeing Granny."

Soon Alicia and Amy arrived at Plantation Manor. Armed with a box of cookies and a backpack full of Barbies, the cookie team swung open the door, ready to make someone's day brighter. Alicia looked around for her grandmother, but she wasn't in her usual waiting spot in the foyer. Alicia approached the nurse's station, trying not to sound alarmed, in spite of the sudden knot in her stomach. "Good morning," she said, "I didn't see my grandmother, Mrs. Hacker. Do you know if she's in her room?"

The nurse looked down at Amy and back at Alicia. The deliberate eye contact was all Alicia needed to tell her things were not right.

"Good morning, Alicia."

Alicia could tell the thoughtful nurse was keeping her tone light to protect Amy.

"We called you and your mother, but you had apparently already left. Your grandmother had a bit of a rough night. She's running a little fever, and the doctor would like to put her in the hospital."

Alicia took a deep breath as she absorbed this new information.

"Mommy, let's go see Granny." Amy was tugging at Alicia's leg again, not comprehending the reason for delay. "She's probably waiting for us to pass out our cookies."

Alicia spoke again to the nurse, asking more with her eyes than she could with her words. "Should we go on in to see her?"

"I think so," the nurse responded. "She's just resting until the ambulance comes to take her to the hospital."

Amy squatted down to meet her eager daughter at eye level. "Amy, Granny's not feeling well today. She won't be able to walk around with us as we deliver the cookies. The doctor is going to take her to the hospital so she can get better and come back to help us. We can go see her, but we have to be a little quieter than usual. OK?"

"OK."

"OK, let's go." Alicia turned and headed toward her grandmother's room, but Amy took off in the opposite direction.

"Whoa, missy," Alicia gently grabbed her daughter's arm and tickled her stomach. "Granny's room is this way."

"But what about the cookies? Everyone's waiting

for them and for us to go and make them smile."

Alicia caught her breath as she looked at her innocent but thoughtful daughter. *Just like Granny—she'd be so proud.* Her throat clenched as she tried to hold back emotions her little girl wouldn't yet understand. "You're right, Amy." She swallowed hard. "Let's pass some out on the way to Granny's room."

Amy giggled as she took the cookie box from her mom and headed toward an older woman in a wheelchair. Alicia could barely hold back her tears as she watched a legacy in action. Amy opened the box, took out a cookie, and handed it to the woman. "Do you know Granny?" Alicia heard Amy say. "She lives here now. She taught my mommy how to make these cookies so we could bring you one. I hope you like it."

The woman's face brightened as she took the cookie and patted Amy on the head, and Alicia was taken back thirty years to the many times she'd had similar interactions. She remembered feeling the warmth of her grandmother's smile that communicated love and pride in her.

"See my backpack?" Alicia heard Amy tell her new friend. "My Barbies are in here. I'm going to leave one with Granny to keep her company when I have to go to school."

The wrinkled lady in the wheelchair had tears glistening in her eyes as she spoke softly to Amy. "I think your Granny will love to have a Barbie to keep her company. You are a very thoughtful granddaughter." She reached out to give Amy a hug. "Thank you for the cookie. You've made my day."

As Alicia watched Amy walk proudly back to her, she knew this was one tradition worth keeping.

Look for these other great Hugs™ books

I Will
See
You in
Heaven

Friar Jack Wintz

PARACLETE PRESS
BREWSTER, MASSACHUSETTS

I Will See You in Heaven

2011 Third and Fourth Printing
2010 First and Second Printing

Copyright © 2010 by Jack Wintz

ISBN: 978-1-55725-732-1

Unless otherwise noted all scriptural references are taken from the *New Revised Standard Version of the Bible*, copyright 1989, 1995 by the Division of Christian Education of the National Council of Churches of Christ in the United States of America and are used by permission. All rights reserved.

Scriptural references marked NAB are taken from the *New American Bible with Revised New Testament and Revised Psalms* © 1991, 1986, 1970 Confraternity of Christian Doctrine, Washington, D.C., and are used by permission. All Rights Reserved. No part of the *New American Bible* may be reproduced in any form without permission in writing from the copyright owner.

Scriptural references marked NAB 1986 in this work are taken from the *New American Bible with Revised New Testament* © 1986, 1970 Confraternity of Christian Doctrine, Washington, D.C., and are used by permission of the copyright owner. All Rights Reserved. No part of the *New American Bible* may be reproduced in any form without permission in writing from the copyright owner.

Scriptural references marked JB are taken from *The Jerusalem Bible* © 1966 by Darton Longman & Todd Ltd and Doubleday and Company Ltd. Used by permission. All rights reserved.

Library of Congress Cataloging-in-Publication Data

Wintz, Jack. I will see you in heaven / Jack Wintz.

p. cm.

ISBN 978-1-55725-732-1

1. Animals—Religious aspects—Christianity. 2. Pets—Religious aspects—Christianity. 3. Future life—Christianity. I. Title. BT746.W55 2010

231.7—dc22   2009053415

10 9 8 7 6 5 4

All rights reserved. No portion of this book may be reproduced, stored in an electronic retrieval system, or transmitted in any form or by any means—electronic, mechanical, photocopy, recording, or any other—except for brief quotations in printed reviews, without the prior permission of the publisher.

Published by Paraclete Press
Brewster, Massachusetts
www.paracletepress.com

*This book is written for
the millions of people
who love their animal companions.
All may find inspiration here.*

I Will See You in Heaven is also designed to help those who have recently lost a pet by keeping it in loving remembrance. You may want to use the following Presentation Page.

Presented to

_____

By _____

In Loving Remembrance of

_____

On This Day

_____

Contents

Introduction

We have a deep desire to know if we will see our pets again, and all the other lovely creatures alongside whom we now inhabit this planet. What will become of them after they die?

A friend of mine once told me the following story:

Anne lives in Cincinnati, where a few years ago she faced the important questions of death and eternity as she was present at the death of her dearly loved dog, Miss Daisy. Anne had befriended Miss Daisy ten years earlier when the dog, of mixed Spaniel origin, was barely one year old. With the help of her adult son, Anne rescued Miss Daisy from Cincinnati's inner city.

"I would see her wandering around the neighborhood where I worked at an elementary school," Anne told me. "I came to realize that she was obviously a stray and lost—and she was adorable! I took cans of tuna to the area where Miss Daisy hung out, but she was very afraid of people and wouldn't approach the tuna till she was left alone. My rescue attempts went on for many months."

In time, Anne was successful in winning Miss Daisy's confidence and was able to take her to her home.

"Miss Daisy was still very shy," Anne told me, "but she eventually became a loyal and loving member of our family. Realizing that Miss Daisy needed a companion, I went to the dog pound and came home with a dog named Andy. For ten years or so, Miss Daisy and Andy were very happy companions, and both became cherished members of the family. But I became especially attached to Miss Daisy.

"Eventually, Miss Daisy became ill, and we had to make the very difficult decision to have her 'put down.' My son and I took her to the veterinarian so he could put her to sleep. We wanted the vet to come out to our car so Miss Daisy would be in familiar surroundings and we could be holding her, but he refused our request. So we had to take her inside. We laid her on the vet's table on her special blanket. We petted Miss Daisy gently and spoke softly to her as the vet got everything ready to give her the injection. Miss Daisy lay there quietly for a few seconds, and then, just before the injection took effect, she lifted her head and looked directly into my eyes. I can still see that look. It was as if she knew what was going on and she was saying good-bye."

Anne recalls how her heart melted, and to this day tears come to her eyes when she remembers that scene. "I still miss the loving pet who had been my dear friend for so many years. *I know I will see Miss Daisy again!"*

I'm sure that most of us have our own memories of being profoundly grief-stricken at the death of a beloved pet. These are not childish concerns, but the mature reflections of loving Christians.

Many of us prefer to pose the question "Will I see my dog in heaven?" in broader spiritual terms. There is more involved in this question than simply wondering if we will ever be reunited with a loved animal. For instance, does God's plan of salvation include only humans, or does it include animals, too? In even broader terms, does God intend the *whole* created world to be saved?

As a Franciscan friar for over fifty years, I am familiar with the stories of St. Francis of Assisi and his close relationship with animals, and these stories have informed the way that I view these things. Perhaps you've heard the stories of this brown-robed friar preaching to the birds, releasing Brother

Rabbit from a trap, or letting Sister Raven serve as his "alarm clock" to awaken him for early morning prayer. I've known for a long time that historians have credited Francis with composing one of the first great poems in the Italian language—a poem, or hymn, usually entitled *The Canticle of the Creatures*. In this hymn, sometimes known as *The Canticle of Brother Sun*, Francis invites all his brother and sister creatures to praise their Creator—Brother Sun and Sister Moon, Brother Fire and Sister Water, as well as Sister Earth, our mother, with all her various fruits and vividly colored flowers.

Some thirty years ago I came to the conclusion, which I've never abandoned, that St. Francis came to see that all creatures form one family of creation. Maybe that conclusion is obvious to you, but for me this idea dawned quite gradually. The conviction has grown stronger and stronger, and this book has grown out of that conviction, and explores the implications of it. What would it mean if all creatures were one family? How would it affect us? How would it change our understanding about God, and about how we relate to God and to each other?

Three Prayers
of
Blessing

SCRIPTURE REFLECTION

[Christ] is before all things,
and in him all things hold together. —Col. 1:17

Gather your family and friends together for these blessings
—it is good to have as much of the family of God present as possible.
Insert the name of your animal companion into these prayers.

For Any of God's Creatures

Blessed are you, Lord God,

Maker of all living creatures.

On the fifth and sixth days of creation,

    you called forth fish in the sea,

    birds in the air, and animals on the land.

You inspired St. Francis to call all animals

    his brothers and sisters.

We ask you to bless this animal (these animals)

    gathered about us.

By the power of your love,

    enable him or her (them) to live according to your plan.

May we always praise you for all your beauty in creation.

Blessed are you, Lord our God, in all your creatures.

Amen.

For One or More Sick Creatures

Heavenly Creator,

you made all things for your glory

  and made us caretakers of this creature

  (these creatures) under our care.

Restore to health and strength this animal

  (this pet) that you have entrusted to us.

Keep this animal (this pet)

  always under your loving protection.

Blessed are you, Lord God,

And holy is your name for ever and ever. Amen.

For an Animal That Has Died or Is About to Die

Loving God,

our beloved pet and companion, (name),

is on its final journey.

We will miss (name) dearly

because of the joy and affection

(name) has given to us.

Bless (name) and give him/her peace.

May your care for (name) never die.

We thank you for the gift

that (name) has been to us.

Give us hope that in your great kindness

you may restore (name) in your heavenly kingdom

according to your wisdom, which goes

beyond our human understanding. Amen.

1
And It Was Very Good

In the earliest verses of Genesis, darkness covered everything until God created light to separate the darkness from the light. "And God saw that the light was good."

Soon we read that God separated the earth from the seas. "And God saw that it was good." Then God added vegetation, plants, trees, and fruit. "And God saw that it was good." On the fourth day, God put two great lights in the sky: the greater light to rule the day and the lesser light to rule the night, thus separating light from darkness. "And God saw that it was good." These two great lights, which St. Francis would call "Brother Sun" and "Sister Moon," have contributed enormously to the well-being and enjoyment of God's creatures.

On the fifth day, God created sea monsters and birds of all kinds. "And God saw that it was good." On the sixth day, God made land creatures of every kind: "cattle and creeping things and wild animals of the earth of every kind. And God saw that it was good." Also on the sixth day, God made human beings, saying, "Let us make humankind in our image, according to our likeness; and let them have dominion over the fish of the sea, and over the birds of the air, and over the cattle, and over all the wild animals of the earth."

Finally, in Genesis 1:31, "God saw everything that he had made, and indeed, it was very good." This "very good" label, which God places upon both human and nonhuman creatures, seems to be an argument for God's desire to have *both* classes of creatures share in the original Garden of Paradise, where peace and harmony reigned between God and human beings, upon creature and creature. Certainly, God is not going to create—and then ignore—what he perceives as "very good" creatures!

God does *everything* out of love, and this includes the creation of our world. God's words to the people of Israel in Jeremiah 31:3 also come to mind: "I have loved you with an everlasting love." The Psalms, too, remind us that God's "steadfast love endures forever." In Psalm 136 alone, the refrain "his steadfast love endures forever" is repeated twenty-five times.

Our God is a God of overflowing love, goodness, and beauty who is ready to give over everything to those he loves. This goodness is reflected in the whole family of creation. When God says of any creature, whether human or nonhuman, that it is "good" or "very good," it is not simply a matter of moral goodness. The creature also has an inherent goodness and beauty—a beauty that reflects God, who is Beauty itself. Surely the Creator would not suddenly stop loving and caring for the creatures he had put into existence with so much care.

2
The Happiness Principle

In the original picture we have of the Garden of Eden before the fall, Adam and Eve and all the creatures are living together happily in peace and harmony in the presence of a loving God—a wonderful and insightful glimpse of the paradise that is to come.

It makes sense to me that the same loving Creator who arranged for these animals and other nonhuman creatures to enjoy happiness in the original Garden would not want to exclude them from the *final* paradise. If they were happy and enjoying God's presence, according to their abilities, in that first Garden, God would want them to be happy and enjoy the same in the restored garden.

Father Don Miller, a Franciscan colleague of mine, recently told me a sad story from his childhood. Don's dog Boots, a young German Shepherd, was tragically killed by a car he had been chasing.

"I was devastated," recalls Don, who was nine years old at the time. "On the verge of tears, I asked my parents: 'Is Boots in heaven and will I see him there some day?'

"This little episode happened in Peoria, Illinois, and my parents took me downtown to Sacred Heart Church to talk with Father Baldwin Schulte, the Franciscan pastor there. I asked Fr. Baldwin whether I would see Boots in heaven. He thought for a moment, and then he turned to me and said: 'Yes, you will see your dog in heaven—if that is what it takes to make you happy.' "

Don reflects, "Now as I look back as an adult, I believe Fr. Baldwin's answer was very wise. Instead of giving me a lot of theology, he basically said that in heaven God will see to it that all who live there are supremely happy. It was a very sound and sensitive answer for me at that time. Once we pass on to the next life and see God face to face, as the glorious source of all that exists, those kinds of questions may not seem so important."

Just as the original Creation was very good with animals as a part of it, so too, it seems, our future lives will be very good and will include animals. No one should presume to tell you or me that we will never again see our pets that died many years ago.

I recall learning in my theology classes that in God there is no past, present, or future. There is only an "eternal now." Who can say, therefore, that the God who created all things does not hold in memory all the creatures God has ever made? They were created as good, all of creation was very good together, and there's no reason why that should change in the eternal future.

The creation story in Genesis says nothing about the future, only about those initial moments when all things were made. But we wonder what will happen in the afterlife—in the new heaven and the new earth that is to come? This is a big-time mystery. There are many things about our future paradise that surpass human understanding. We simply do not know what awaits us in heaven. As St. Paul tells the Corinthians, "We teach what scripture calls: *the things that no eye has seen and no ear has heard, things beyond the mind of man, all that God has prepared for those who love him*" (1 Cor. 2:9 JB).

The Garden of Eden is not only a story of the way the world was created; it is also a metaphor for the final paradise that our loving Creator envisioned before time began.

3
Blessing the Animals

When I try to visualize the final paradise in which animals and humans live together in peace and harmony, I often think of animal blessings that I have taken part in. This is particularly true on the Feast Day of St. Francis, when churches all over the world hold "Blessing of the Animals" services, in which creatures are invited into the sanctuary and offered special blessings as members of God's family. An ideal alternative setting for such a ceremony is a park or a church courtyard with lots of trees and flowers in it and perhaps a fountain or a pool of water.

Ironically, when people bring their pets from different parts of town, there can be disharmony and trouble. Dogs start barking at cats and people struggle to keep animals from fighting, growling, and hissing. But often in my experience, once the blessings begin, a spirit of harmony and peace prevails among pets and people.

Many Christians believe that nonhuman creatures do not have a place in heaven. The reasoning seems to go like this: life with God after death is only possible for human beings who have received the gift of new life with God through baptism. Only humans have intelligence and free will and thus have the capacity to enjoy fullness of life in heaven. Similarly, animals and other nonhuman creatures do not have human souls and are thus excluded from heaven, according to this mindset.

My comment is this: when we consider the story of Adam and Eve before their disobedience, and we look at the animals, the birds, the fish, the trees and plants in the Garden of Eden, they all seem to be in harmonious and happy relationship with God and with Adam and Eve.

True, the nonhuman creatures do not have human souls, but they obviously have some kind of principle of life in order to do the things they do. An animal that shows affection and loyalty, for example, surely has some kind of "soul" or inner light that allows it to enjoy life and give great joy to its caretakers. A bird that sings a beautiful melody contributes to the world of art and, by reflecting the beauty of its Maker, gives us a bit of heaven in the process. There are a lot of things we just don't know about life with God, and one of these things is how nonhumans participate in that life.

One thing we *do* know from the Genesis stories is that animals, plants, and other creatures found happiness in the first Paradise. Why then would God—or anyone else—want to exclude them from the paradise that is yet to come? Just as we find clues in the book of Genesis that God wants animals and other nonhuman creatures to share such joys, so we will also, in the chapters ahead, find clues in other books of Scripture, and elsewhere, that reveal this same desire on the part of God.

For more than thirty-six years, I have worked as a writer and editor for *St. Anthony Messenger*, a national Catholic magazine published by the Franciscan friars of Cincinnati. In our July 2003 issue, we printed an article that I wrote entitled "Will I See My Little Doggy in Heaven?" The article generated a lively reaction from our readers, and we received a larger than usual number of letters, suggesting that the topic of animals in heaven is a live one. I am happy to share with you a letter published two months later in our September issue of that year:

Dear editors:

I am still jumping up and down over the article about animals in heaven. All observations made by Father Jack are sound references to the fact that God loves all creation and will include all in our heavenly home.

For the past several years, I have organized a "Blessing of the Animals." In 1972, I had written to Mother Teresa [of Calcutta] to ask for a letter of support. She sent one, over her own signature, and I quote: "[Animals] too are created by the same hand of God which created us. As we humans are gifted with intelligence, which the animals lack, it is our duty to protect them and to promote their well-being. We also owe it to them as they serve us with such docility and loyalty."

I think Mother Teresa says all there is to say about the sacredness of the animal kingdom.

From Marlene,
Louisville, KY

4
Noah, the Ark, and the Dove

The story of Noah and the ark is simple—it couldn't be more familiar, could it? Most of us knew it as very young children. But our understanding grows, just as our bodies do.

The ark is a wonderful symbol of God's desire to save the whole family of creation. This story makes it apparent that God's plan is not to save humankind apart from other creatures. We are all in the same boat! As St. Paul writes to the Romans (8:22 NAB), "All creation is groaning" for its liberation.

Because of the widespread wickedness at that time, God tells Noah that he is going to destroy everything living on the earth as well as the earth itself. God instructs Noah to build a huge ark with a roof, three decks, a door on the side, and many other specifications.

I am amazed at God's care and solicitude for *all* the creatures in the ark, and this applies to the animals also. God shows his love and care in bringing aboard the ark "every kind" of creature (wanting no species to go extinct) and that they should be "male and female" alike (insuring the continuation and propagation of each of these species). God doesn't want Noah to pack them in the back of a big truck and rush them off to some safe place. No, God wants Noah to be more caring about the details, as well as about all these brother and sister creatures.

"Then the Lord said to Noah, 'Go into the ark, you and all your household, for I have seen that you alone are righteous before me in this generation'" (Gen. 7:1). When we stop to see what's happening, we find that God's care focuses not only upon the human family but also upon the whole family of creation. The animals and other creatures are now part of Noah's "household" and in his care, just as they had been under God's loving care from the beginning. To imitate the broad solicitude of our Creator, a good human leader must care not only for other human beings, but also for the earth and for the wider family of creation.

As children who have heard the story well know, it rained for forty days and forty nights. We also recall that after the rain stopped, Noah opened the window of the ark and sent out a dove to see if the waters had subsided, but since the dove had no place to land, it returned to the ark. Noah waited seven days, and sent the dove out again. This time the dove came back in the evening with an olive leaf. This assured Noah that the waters were subsiding. After waiting another seven days, he sent out the dove, and this time the dove did not return, indicating that the flood was over. Noah and his wife and their three sons and their wives—and all the animals—had survived. All were safe.

But take a closer look at that dove. The episode of Noah and the dove is a little story within the bigger story, and reinforces the idea that God's plan is not to save the humans apart from the other creatures. Humans and other creatures are actually meant to help one another reach our common salvation. What might it mean, if we came to understand humans and animals as helping each other on the way to union with God?

5
Animals and God's Will

We can find many other instances in the Bible (and in our own lives) in which God's creatures collaborate with us in our journey toward salvation and in carrying out God's designs. Consider, for example, the donkey in the Gospels that carried Christ during his triumphal entry into Jerusalem (see Lk. 19:29–38).

Or think of an occasion in your own life—when you see a beautiful flower on a spring day, for example, and it lifts your heart to praise your Creator.

Or consider how often in the book of Psalms the psalmist, upon seeing the sun and moon and shining stars and other beautiful creatures, is inspired to invite these creatures to join the human family in singing God's praises, drawing us all closer to our Creator and our God-given destiny (see Ps. 148).

But let's get back to the bigger story of Noah. That story is not yet finished, even though the flood has gone away. After the waters subsided and dried up, Noah's household, along with all the other creatures, left the ark.

> Then Noah built an altar to the Lord, and took of every clean animal and of every clean bird, and offered burnt offerings on the altar. And when the Lord smelled the pleasing odor, the Lord said in his heart, "I will never again curse the ground because

of humankind . . . nor will I ever again destroy every living creature as I have done." (Gen. 8:20–21)

At this point, "God blessed Noah and his sons, and said to them, 'Be fruitful and multiply, and fill the earth'" (Gen. 9:1). Interestingly, this is exactly what God told the first man and woman immediately after God created them "in his image" in Genesis 1. Apparently, God is telling Noah and his sons (and their wives, obviously) that this is a "new creation" and a "second chance."

This time God backs up his pledge, to never again destroy human beings and other living creatures, with a solemn covenant. Note that the covenant is made not only with Noah and his descendants but also *with the other living creatures*, the animals and birds that had been on the ark. This suggests that those other creatures communicate with God, in their own ways, in ways that may be similar and equivalent to our own communications.

In God's own words, "I establish my covenant with you, that never again shall all flesh be cut off by the waters of a flood, and never again shall there be a flood to destroy the earth" (Gen. 9:11). As if to show how serious this pledge is, God introduces a dramatic sign—the rainbow. "God said, 'This is the sign of the covenant that I make between me and you and every living creature that is with you, for all future generations: I have set my bow in the clouds, and it shall be sign between me and the earth'" (Gen. 9:12–13).

Thus in the story of Noah and the ark, there is no way to mistake that God's plan is to save the human family along with the rest of creation. And God backs this plan up with a covenant—which specifically includes "every living creature." God punctuates this pledge with the rainbow, a sign of hope, arching across the whole family of creation.

6
Jonah and the Whale

Do you remember the story? There is a furious storm at sea. The sailors throw Jonah into the raging water when they discover that Jonah caused the storm. The seas calm. There is a lesson to be "taken away" from the story into our lives.

Jonah had tried to run far away from the task God had asked of him: to preach to the city of Nineveh, the capital city of the Assyrians. The Assyrians were the longtime enemies of the Israelites. It is no surprise then that the Israelites, Jonah among them, felt very little love for the Ninevites. Jonah was not at all pleased that God's saving love included the likes of them. (You may find it interesting to know that the ruins of ancient Nineveh can still be seen today across the Tigris River opposite Mosul in northern Iraq.)

God arranged for a big fish to swallow Jonah. He was in the belly of the fish "three days and three nights." He pleaded for the Lord to deliver him. He offered thanks and pledged obedience to the Lord, saying, "'What I have vowed I will pay. Deliverance belongs to the Lord!' Then the Lord spoke to the fish, and it spewed Jonah out upon the dry land" (2:9–10).

The story of Jonah is a parable of God's all-embracing love. It is amazing to realize that once again *even the animals are included in God's saving plan*. When Jonah proclaimed to the people of Nineveh, "Forty days more and Nineveh will be overthrown," the people and the king of Nineveh were very responsive. "[The king] rose from his throne, removed his robe, covered himself with sackcloth [rough clothing], and sat in ashes" (3:6). Then the king made a decree: "No human being or animal, no herd or flock, shall taste anything. They shall not feed, nor shall they drink water. Human beings and animals shall be covered in sackcloth, and they shall cry mightily to God. All shall turn from their evil ways and from the violence that is in their hands" (3:7–8).

When God saw that the people *and* the animals turned from their evil ways, God changed his mind about the calamity that was to befall the city and withheld all punishment. Jonah became very angry because God's mercy and forgiveness extended beyond the chosen people and included their enemies, the people of Nineveh. Jonah confessed that it was precisely the idea of God's merciful and inclusive love that drove him to flee from God's request that he preach to the people of Nineveh in the first place. Now, no doubt, it made Jonah angrier to know that God wanted to save *even the animals*.

Jonah then went outside the city and made a hut for himself. He sat there waiting to see what would happen to the city. God, meanwhile, provided a bush for Jonah to help shade his head. For this Jonah was grateful. But the next day God had a worm attack the bush, causing it to wither. When the sun rose and beat down on Jonah's head, Jonah asked that he might die, saying, "It is better for me to die than to live" (4:8).

God asked Jonah whether it is right for him "to be angry about the bush." Jonah replied, "Yes, angry enough to die" (4:9). To this the Lord replied,

> You are concerned about the bush, for which you did not labor and which you did not grow; it came into being in a night and perished in a night. And should I not be concerned about Nineveh, that great city, in which there are more than a hundred and twenty thousand persons who do not know their right hand from their left, and also many animals?" (4:10–11).

This intriguing question ends the story: God's point seems to be that, if Jonah can throw a big snit about a little bush for which Jonah did not even lift his little finger, why should not the loving Creator of the universe be concerned about the great city of Nineveh and all the human beings and animals that live there?

Just as in the story of Noah and the ark, when a dove was used by Noah to assist in God's plan to save the whole family of creation, so now in this amazing, inspired story of Jonah, we see a big fish taking a similar role. The fish plays a key function in helping the reluctant Jonah carry out God's plan to save Nineveh. Again, this is an example of a creature helping us on our way to salvation. We are a part of the Creation, not *apart from* it.

God uses a bush and a worm to lead the narrow-minded Jonah to a better understanding of the inclusive nature of God's saving love. Human beings and other creatures are meant to help each other in our common journey toward our future life with God.

Animals can teach us a lot about rising above our narrow-mindedness and intolerance. We see dogs, cats, and other pets showing great affection to their owners, whether these owners be rich or poor, black or white, beautiful or disfigured, healthy or sick. I have a clear memory of a volunteer coming regularly to a nursing home a few years ago with a young Collie to visit my mother and other residents of that home. That dog certainly gave great comfort to my mom, who was coping with cancer at the time. The dog, with the full approval of the volunteer, had no qualms whatsoever about lying alongside my ninety-four-year-old mother as she lay propped up in bed. She was so happy to pet and enjoy this wonderful creature on her final journey toward life with God.

We have much to learn about God's inclusive love, and about *our* role in collaborating respectfully with other creatures as we go on our way to fulfill our Creator's holy designs.

7
Creatures Praise Our Creator

In the book of Psalms we find prayers in which human beings invite other creatures to praise God along with them. The clear impression in these prayers is that the nonhuman creatures are meant to participate in our prayerful journey into the presence of God. These are often inclusive prayers addressed to a wide range of God's creation: sun and moon, trees, animals, birds, sea monsters, as well as to a variety of people.

Psalm 148 is a dramatic example of this. In the New American Bible (1986 edition), this psalm bears the awesome title: "Hymn of All Creation to the Almighty Creator." I invite you to read—or better, to pray—this hymn, which includes a broad spectrum of God's creatures:

PSALM 148
Hymn of All Creation to the Almighty Creator

I. Praise the LORD from the heavens;
praise him in the heights.
Praise him, all you angels;
praise him, all you his host.
Praise him, sun and moon;
praise him, all you shining stars.
Praise him, you highest heavens,
and you waters above the heavens.

Let them praise the name of the LORD,

for he commanded and they were created;

He established them forever and ever;

he gave them a duty which shall not pass away.

II. Praise the LORD from the earth,

you sea monsters and all depths;

Fire and hail, snow and mist,

storm winds that fulfill his word;

You mountains and all you hills,

you fruit trees and all you cedars;

You wild beasts and all tame animals,

you creeping things and you winged foul.

III. Let the kings of the earth and all peoples,

the princes and all the judges of the earth,

Young men too, and maidens,

old men and boys,

Praise the name of the LORD,

for his name alone is exalted;

His majesty is above earth and heaven,

and he has lifted up the horn of his people.

Be this his praise from all his faithful ones,

from the children of Israel, the people close to him.

Alleluia. (NAB 1986)

In the first two stanzas, nonhuman creatures in heaven, sea, and earth are praising God. And in the final stanza, those praising God are all human beings. The picture we have is of the combined family of creation joined in praising God together. Doesn't that seem to be the way that God wills it? God is not seeking praise solely from the *human* part of the family, but from the *whole* family of creation.

Just as in the story of the ark and the great flood, in which Noah and his family along with the larger family of nonhuman creatures are saved together, so it is in the case of this hymn. All creatures are praising God together. *We are all in the same boat*, once again, seeking a share in God's mercy and love, and someday, final happiness in the restored garden.

8
The Song of St. Francis

The broad strokes of his life are familiar to most. St. Francis was born in 1182 in the Umbrian town of Assisi. The son of a prosperous cloth merchant, Francis was a carefree and generous youth.

His companions dubbed him the "King of Revels." He loved the good life and partying with his friends. All the while, however, he dreamed of becoming a knight and achieving glory on the battlefield. The opportunity soon arrived and Francis rode off as a knight of Assisi to fight against the neighboring town of Perugia.

Assisi, however, was roundly defeated in its very first skirmish, and Francis was captured and became a prisoner of war. It was a bitter blow for this idealistic young man of twenty-one. Francis spent a year in prison and returned home to Assisi a broken man.

Yet a plan seemed to be unfolding. While praying alone one day before a crucifix in the abandoned chapel of San Damiano located down the hill from Assisi, Francis heard these words coming from the cross: "Francis, repair my house, which is falling into ruin." The saint realized only later that it was a larger house, the Christian Church itself, that Christ was calling him to rebuild.

Another dramatic sign of Francis's new direction came through his meeting with a leper on the road. Francis was inspired to dismount his horse and warmly embrace and kiss the leper. Later Francis confessed in his *Testament* that "[w]hat had seemed bitter to me [an encounter with leprosy] was turned into sweetness of soul and body." Francis realized that he had actually embraced his Lord, Jesus Christ.

Soon Francis found himself living among lepers and humbly caring for them. Others, seeing Francis joyfully ministering to the lepers and to other outcasts, asked to join Francis in his ministry to the poor. These followers would soon grow into a brotherhood, and in 1209, Pope Innocent III approved the Franciscan way of life.

But this early information about the life of St. Francis does not tell us about another very important aspect of Francis's life, namely his great admiration for the wonders of nature and the marvelous creatures God placed on earth to accompany us on our journey to God. This brings us to St. Francis's great *Canticle of the Creatures*. This hymn, or song of praise to our Creator, was composed very much in the spirit of Psalm 148 discussed in the previous chapter.

This song is also known as *The Canticle of Brother Sun.* In it Francis gives the title of "Brother" and "Sister" to the various creatures, emphasizing as best he could that we all form *one family of creation* under one loving "Father." "Sister" and "Brother," of course, are familial terms that people formerly only used for fellow humans.

Francis had a strong sense, which he probably learned from the Old Testament psalms and hymns, that we are not meant to journey to God alone, in proud isolation from our brother and sister creatures. Indeed, Francis would have regularly encountered these psalms and hymns in his liturgical prayers. For example, he would have certainly recited with frequency the following verses from the book of Daniel:

> Sun and moon, bless the Lord;
>   praise and exalt him above all forever.
> Stars of heaven, bless the Lord;
>   praise and exalt him above all forever.
> Every shower and dew, bless the Lord;
>   praise and exalt him above all forever.

All you winds, bless the Lord;

    praise and exalt him above all forever.

Fire and heat, bless the Lord;

    praise and exalt him above all forever. (3:62–66 NAB)

One can easily imagine Francis borrowing these words and phrases and using them in his *Canticle of the Creatures*. Just as in the case of the psalms and hymns of the Hebrew Scriptures, Francis invites us in his exuberant *Canticle* to form one family with these creatures and to sing out in one symphony of praise to our common Creator.

Here is a slightly condensed version of St. Francis's famous song:

The Canticle of the Creatures

Most high, all-powerful, all-good Lord!

    All praise is yours, all glory, all honor,

    and all blessing.

To you alone, Most High, do they belong.

    No mortal lips are worthy

    to pronounce your name.

All praise be yours, my Lord,
  through all that you have made,
And first my lord Brother Sun,
    who brings the day;
    and light you give to us through him.
    How beautiful is he,
    how radiant in all his splendor!
    Of you, Most High, he bears the likeness.
All praise be yours, my Lord,
  through Sister Moon and Stars,
    in the heavens you have made them, bright
    and precious and fair.
All praise be yours, my Lord,
  through Brothers Wind and Air,
    and fair and stormy, all the weather's moods,
    by which you cherish all that you have made.
All praise be yours, my Lord, through Sister Water,
    so useful, lowly, precious, and pure.

All praise be yours, my Lord, through Brother Fire,

> through whom you brighten up the night.

> How beautiful is he, how merry!

> Full of power and strength.

All praise be yours, my Lord,

> through Sister Earth, our mother,

>> who feeds us in her sovereignty and produces

>> various fruits and colored flowers and herbs. . . .

Praise and bless my Lord, and give him thanks,

> And serve him with great humility.

9
St. Francis and the Creatures

Just as we find a spirit of great care and reverence for the creatures in St. Francis's *Canticle,* so we find in Francis's daily life the same spirit of reverence for every creature he encountered along his way.

Francis's care for creation even extended to earthworms he saw on the roadway. He would carefully pick them up and place them on the side of the road where they would be out of harm's way. Francis saw the goodness and beauty of God in the sunset or in a gurgling stream. He was in awe of the butterfly as well as the cricket.

"Where the modern cynic sees something 'bug-like' in everything that exists," observed the German writer-philosopher Max Scheler, "St. Francis saw even in a bug the sacredness of life."

There are many other popular stories about St. Francis and other creatures.

One day a rabbit was brought to him by a brother who had found it caught in a trap. Francis admonished the rabbit to be more careful in the future. Releasing the rabbit from the trap, Francis sat it on the ground and told it to go its way. But the rabbit just hopped back to Francis and sat on his lap, desiring to stay close to him. Francis carried the rabbit into the woods and set it free. The rabbit simply followed Francis back to where he was seated and jumped onto his lap again.

Finally Francis asked one of his brothers to take the rabbit deep into the forest and let it go. This time it worked; the rabbit remained content there. Such episodes were always happening to Francis, who saw this as an opportunity to give praise to God.

Francis also made friends with fish. Once, he was crossing a lake with a fisherman, who caught a nice-sized fish and gave it to Francis as a gift. Francis, however, simply warned the fish not to get caught again and placed it back in the water.

This brings us to the well-known legend of Francis and a fierce wolf that had been terrorizing the village of Gubbio. The wolf had attacked and even killed some of the townspeople. Through the intervention of Francis, the townspeople promised to feed the wolf, if the wolf stopped its violent attacks. Francis brought the conflict to a peaceful solution. He was the sort of person—extraordinarily rare but possible—who could communicate with creatures, because he was sensitive to them and to their needs.

Finally we have the famous story of Francis's preaching to the birds. Sometimes people hear this story out of its proper context. This episode was not a fanciful event. We shouldn't make it into something magical, unrelated to real life.

In reading the story again recently, I was puzzled by the way that Francis's biographer St. Bonaventure positioned this famous story in his *Life of St. Francis*. He placed the story right at the point in Francis's life where he is struggling with a deep personal dilemma: should he retire from the world and devote himself entirely to prayer, or should he continue traveling about as a preacher of the gospel? To answer this question, Francis sent brothers to seek the advice of two trusted colleagues: Brother Sylvester and St. Clare. Word came back quickly from both Sylvester and Clare that it was their clear judgment that God wanted Francis to keep proclaiming the Good News of God's saving love. No sooner did Francis hear their response than he immediately stood up, and in the words of Bonaventure, "without the slightest delay he took to the roads to carry out the divine command" with great fervor.

We might expect Francis to go running off to the nearest village to begin preaching the gospel to the people gathered there. But where does Francis actually go? His very next stop, according to Bonaventure, is this: "He came to a spot where a large flock of birds of various kinds had come together. When God's saint saw them, he quickly ran to the spot and greeted them as if they were endowed with reason. . . ."

He went right up to them and solicitously urged them to listen to the word of God, saying, "Oh birds, my brothers [and sisters], you have a great obligation to praise your Creator, who clothed you in feathers and gave you wings to fly with, provided you with pure air and cares for you without any worry on your part. . . ." The birds showed their joy in a remarkable fashion: They began to stretch their necks, extend their wings, open their beaks, and gaze at him attentively.

He went through their midst with amazing fervor of spirit, brushing against them with his tunic. Yet none of them moved from the spot until the man of God made the sign of the cross and gave them permission to leave; then they all flew away together. His companions waiting on the road saw all these things. When he returned to them, that pure and simple man began to accuse himself of negligence because he had not preached to the birds before.

During his life, St. Francis had more than one mystical experience in which Jesus revealed himself as a God of overflowing goodness and love who would lay down his own life for Francis. The same incredible goodness that Francis saw in God he saw also in creatures. That is why he could compose a *Canticle of the Creatures* that not only praises the Creator as good in its opening line ("Most high, all-powerful, all-good Lord!") but also describes the creatures with similar words: "beautiful," "radiant," "bright," "precious and fair"—words shining with the glory and goodness of God.

Francis's amazement at God's goodness is reflected time and again in his style of prayer. In a prayer from his *Praises before the Office*, Francis suddenly begins repeating, if not babbling, the word *good*, as if intoxicated by it. He prays:

All powerful, all holy, most high and supreme God,
sovereign good, all good,
every good, you who alone
are good, it is to you we must give all praise,
all glory, all thanks, all honor, all blessing;
to you we must refer
all good always. Amen.

Artists, too, have often expressed this kind of goodness and reverence in their artistic representations of St. Francis and his fellow creatures. I think of the great painter Giotto and his famous thirteenth-century fresco of *St. Francis Preaching to the Birds* that is located in the Upper Basilica of St. Francis in Assisi. In this painting, Francis and another friar companion are standing in front of a tree and a large group of birds are scattered on the ground before Francis and looking intently toward him. Francis's right hand is raised in blessing as he bends slightly before them in a posture of gentle reverence and wonder before the mystery of God's creation. The whole scene exudes a sense of the goodness of God.

I think also of present-day artists who have sculpted popular statues of St. Francis that stand in our flower gardens or on our birdbaths. I think of greeting cards and T-shirts showing images of Francis with birds flying around his head or with a rabbit in his arms. Such images inspire us to love and respect all creatures.

St. Francis addressed creatures as "sisters" and "brothers," that is, as equals, not as subjects to be dominated. That is why the humble figure of St. Francis standing on the birdbath or among the shrubs is so right for our day. He truly saw himself as a simple servant and a caretaker of creation—little brother to the birds and the fish and the lowly ivy.

For these reasons and more, Pope John Paul II proclaimed St. Francis of Assisi the patron of ecology in 1979. The pope cited him for being "an example of genuine and deep respect for the integrity of creation." "St. Francis," he added, "invited all creation—animals, plants, natural forces, even Brother Sun and Sister Moon—to give honor and praise to the Lord."

10
Jesus and the World of Creation

Jesus of Nazareth lived his earthly life twelve centuries before St. Francis of Assisi. Long before Francis understood a sense of brotherhood with the rest of creation, Jesus had plunged in and immersed himself in the created world, becoming a *brother to every creature*. This he did through the Incarnation—a breathtaking event that sent rumblings of new life and hope through the entire network of creation.

The Incarnation is the central mystery of Christianity. One thing is very clear: Jesus, as the Divine Word, did not hold himself aloof from the world he had come to save, but literally and wholeheartedly *entered* the family of creation. He did this through his incarnation, his taking human form, his birth at Bethlehem. It's an amazing mystery, because when the Word became flesh in Christ and made his home among us, not only were human beings raised to a new and glorious dignity but all other creatures were as well.

When Jesus walked this earth, he must have perceived that the whole world had been ennobled by his entering into it. Jesus felt at home on this earth, whether on the lakeshore or in the desert, whether walking down a mountainside or crossing a wheat field or sailing across the Sea of Galilee.

In his preaching of the Good News, Jesus delighted in using images from nature, such as the birds of the air and the lilies of the field. He populated his sermons with stories of foxes, pearls, salt, yeast, fig trees, mustard seed, weeds and wheat, moths, and lost sheep. He understood from his profound knowledge of Scripture that all these creatures were blessed and pronounced *good* by the Creator in the beginning.

Jesus used many created things in his saving work, such as wet clay to heal the eyes of a blind man. He used bread and wine, the product of wheat and grapes, to represent his very presence in the Eucharist. We see from examples like this how Jesus incorporated other creatures into his mission of carrying out God's saving plan for the world.

Finally, near the end of Mark's Gospel, in his farewell message to his disciples, Jesus left a strong hint that the whole family of creation was to be included in God's saving work. After his death and resurrection, Jesus tells his disciples: "Go into the whole world and proclaim the gospel to every creature" (Mk. 16:15). Mark does not use the words "to every human being," but "to every creature." Jesus' choice of words suggests that the gospel message will have a saving impact upon the *whole* family of creation, and not simply on the human family.

11
Praying with Creatures

Coming as I do from the Roman Catholic tradition, my fellow worshipers and I are used to liturgies of prayer that rely heavily on a wide and rich spectrum of creatures. On our most solemn feasts, for example, we use fire, clouds of incense, blazing candles, and multicolored flowers.

In our sacramental celebrations, we use bread, wine, water, oil, ashes, and palm branches. We decorate our prayer spaces with stained glass windows, images of lambs, doves, lions, eagles, oxen, and asses. We pray in the company of these creatures day after day in our public worship.

As a Catholic I find it normal to incorporate these brother and sister creatures into my worship. Sacramentality is very much the air we breathe, whether it is a matter of celebrating the Eucharist or public prayers that mention our fellow creatures. Christians of all backgrounds can believe in the inherent sanctity of all these creatures, accepting them as outward signs and "sacraments" of God's presence, goodness, and grace.

One of the prayers we frequently hear the priest say at Mass is:

Father, you are holy indeed and all
creation rightly gives you praise.

I love this prayer. The words express our way of including the whole family of creation in prayer. We can surely find new ways to apply these words to the creatures we invite to accompany us in praising God.

There is a principle in Catholic theology that goes like this in Latin: *lex orandi, lex credendi*. Translated literally, it means, "The law of prayer is the law of belief." An easier-to-understand translation would be:

The way we pray indicates
the way we believe.

May we find more and creative words to express what we believe about this world, and the one to come.

12
The Soul of a Dog

The question—"Will I see my dog (my cat, my rabbit, my gerbil, my parrot, my turtle) in heaven?"—is one that is very close to our hearts. It is important. The question of the future of our beloved pets holds deep emotional importance for us—and it should.

Although I do not have a dog or a pet at this point in my life, I have some experience of caring for animals and feeling emotional ties to them. Let me tell you a story that takes me back many years.

Around 1943, when I was about eight years old, our family had a dog named Toppy, and my older brother, Paul, and I had the responsibility of taking care of him. Toppy was part Beagle and was under our care only for a year or two, because it wasn't long before the poor creature got hit and killed by a car. My brother witnessed the tragic event and ran into our house, crying inconsolably, telling the rest of us the terrible news. I keenly felt that loss.

For weeks and maybe months after his death, I kept expecting to see Toppy come bounding into our backyard where his doghouse had stood—but Toppy never showed up. Obviously, that strong memory, still vividly with me so many years later, is a clear indication of my own grief. So I understand how difficult it is to lose such a loved one.

Let me tell you a more recent story, as well. Magic is a different dog and a different story altogether. Magic came into my life more recently. Her home is in Seattle, Washington, with my sister and brother-in-law, Tese and Bill Neighbor, and their two teenage boys, Josh and Noah. Magic is a Golden Retriever. I knew Magic as a pup, and my fondness for her is renewed often, thanks to visits with the family in Seattle at Christmastime, and sometimes in the summer as well.

About eight years ago the Neighbors invited me to use their cabin while I was working on a writing project. Their cabin is located on the Olympic Peninsula, two or three hours west of Seattle. Tese persuaded me that during my two- or three-week stay at the cabin I might want to babysit for Magic, who was just a pup at the time. Her request had its perks. The cabin with its ample deck sits on a wooded hillside and has a panoramic view of the Hood Canal, part of the intercoastal water system that spreads out from Seattle. The area is rich in natural beauty and wildlife. Two bald eagles often perch atop a tall pine tree that towers over the cabin. Those awesome birds seem to have almost come with the property.

To breathe in all this beauty and bond with this affectionate pup were great blessings for me. Besides feeding and watching over Magic, I took breaks from my writing project and went on happy walks with her on scenic forest paths along the canal.

As time went on, Magic began living up to her name as a *retriever*. She displayed incredible retrieving skills at the cabin. Somehow Magic learned to retrieve bright green tennis balls thrown off the cabin deck toward the canal that spreads out like a huge lake down below. The cabin's deck must be sixty feet above the surface of the water. To get to the water, Magic had to race down fifteen or so wooden steps connecting the deck to the ground below, then charge some twenty yards down the steep hillside through the shrubs and undergrowth, down twenty more wooden steps to the level of the canal—and finally dash another few yards to reach the water. During one of my summer visits about a decade ago, Magic came to me with a tennis ball clenched in her teeth and dropped it at my feet on the deck, then looked up at me with her bright eyes, as if to say, "Try me out!"

Having played baseball as a teenager, I still have a fairly good arm. After warming up a bit, I threw the ball over the top branches of a row of tall evergreens that partially blocked the view of the canal from spectators on the deck, including

Magic. Magic watched my wind-up and throw quite carefully. Then, after catching only a split-second glimpse of the ball's trajectory, she charged down the steps and hillside and soon plunged into the water below. Amazingly, within two or three minutes she came rushing back onto the deck and dropped the ball at my feet. She looked up at me again with her bright eyes and playful grin. This girl really loves being a retriever, I thought with amazement. And as I soon found out, Magic could keep playing this game for hours.

Happily, another very appealing dog has come into my life within the last year or so—a little white Shih Tzu named Tita. She's as cute as a button and is often a guest at Pleasant Street Friary in Cincinnati's inner city, where I live with five other Franciscan friars. Tita belongs to a friend of Mark, one of the friars with whom I live, and is with us one or two days a week, or even more when her owner is called out of town. She is a hit with everyone because she brings her own brand of joy and affection into the friary.

Jim, one of the other friars, has taught her a few tricks such as rolling over, extending her paw for a "handshake," and standing on her hind legs to ask for a bit of food. Tita sometimes joins us when our small community of friars gathers for the Eucharist. She is always very quiet and reverent during Mass, and some of us enjoy greeting Tita at the "sign of peace." We are happy to have this wonderful fellow creature "praising God" with us at times in our friary. In her own mysterious and "doggy" way, Tita is a little mirror of the goodness and love of God that we celebrate in the Eucharist.

Then there is one more dog that I feel compelled to tell you about, because he brought great peace to my soul three or four years ago. I was visiting some good friends who introduced me to Pippy, a full-grown, chocolate Labrador Retriever. I was seated when they brought the dog into the room. Rather large, he came up close and sat upright directly in front of me. He just sat there in silence, hardly a foot away from my face, looking into my eyes with an expression of gentle sadness. He did this more than once during my visit.

Quite puzzled by what was going on between Pippy and me, I asked Pippy's owners what they thought was happening. My friends, who knew that my mother had died from cancer two or three weeks earlier, told me that Pippy had probably sensed my emotional pain and felt a sympathetic connection with me. That rang true, because my heart had been deeply wrenched by my mother's death, and I could feel a real flow of compassion coming from Pippy. This is a very comforting memory for me. Pippy just sat there and kept looking at me in silence as if to comfort and to say, "I feel your loss."

I know that some people say animals don't have souls. I have no problem agreeing that they don't have exactly the same kind of souls that humans have. But I have a hard time accepting that an animal like Magic or Tita or Pippy does not have a soul.

All of these dogs that I have known and loved also have great intelligence, and an amazing set of instincts. Nobody can say that they don't have mighty hearts, a wonderful sense of play, and great capacities to give and receive affection.

Even if you have trouble seeing that dogs such as these have souls, I hope that you will at least agree that they have received amazing gifts from our Creator.

13
The
Afterlife

In this book I have set forth reasons why I believe that creatures other than humans will find a place in that "new heaven and new earth" that the Bible talks about.

In the creation accounts of Genesis, we have learned that all creatures are good and reflect the goodness of God. It is easy for me to recognize this same goodness not only in the abstract, but also when I think specifically of Toppy, Magic, Tita, Pippy, and other creatures I've come to know.

I have also discussed how belief in Jesus Christ, who entering our created world through the Incarnation, elevates the dignity not only of humans but also of animals. I find it meaningful to apply this elevated dignity to Magic and Tita and to all of our animal companions. The same is true of the principal of sacramentality—the belief that every created thing can be a sign or "sacrament" of the divine. This can certainly apply to our beloved animal friends.

So, then, what about the resurrection of our bodies and the bodies of our beloved animals? Does it make sense to believe that this will happen? This is part of the Christian's hope for heaven.

I would like to answer this question by sharing with you a quote from St. Paul's letter to the Philippians that very recently caught me by surprise: "Our citizenship is in heaven, and from it we also await a savior, the Lord Jesus Christ. He will change our lowly body to conform with his glorified body by the power that enables him also to bring all things into subjection to himself" (Phil. 3:20–21 NAB).

These words caught me by surprise. Paul is assuring us that our true home ("our citizenship") is in heaven. He assures us that our bodies too are destined to rise again and be transformed like Christ's own body. Paul also tells us that Christ, as the Lord of Creation, is able "to bring all things into subjection to himself." He is saying that our Savior somehow contains "all things" in his risen body. Paul seems to be saying that "all things"—whether human, animal, plant, or mineral—are somehow meant to be saved and summed up in the risen Christ.

If we believe, therefore, in these words of St. Paul and in our wider Judeo-Christian vision, I feel we can make a good case for saying: yes, in some mysterious but real way, our animal, plant, and mineral companions, our "brothers" and "sisters," will be with us in the restored Garden of Eden.

In chapter 5 of the book of Revelation, the inspired writer gives us an intriguing description of a vision he saw when he was a prisoner on the Greek island of Patmos. The vision is reminiscent of Psalm 148, because it gives us a glimpse of all creatures of the universe praising God together.

In his vision, John sees God sitting on a glorious throne in heaven. Standing near the throne is Jesus in the form of a lamb. An immense crowd of angels and human beings are also there before God and the Lamb. Here is John's testimony:

> Then I heard every creature in heaven and on earth and under the earth and in the sea, everything in the universe cry out: "To the one who sits on the throne and to the Lamb be blessing and honor, glory and might, forever and ever." (Rev. 5:13 NAB)

What we see here, in the last book of the Bible, is the whole family of creation praising God and the Lamb. We know that the book of Revelation often communicates its message symbolically rather than literally. Whatever way we look at John's vision, however, he seems to be affirming that all creatures of the universe are in the presence of God, and blessing him with "honor and glory . . . forever and ever."

There are several other places in the book of Revelation where there are hopeful Scripture passages about a future paradise, the state of happiness we commonly call heaven, and they all bring my thoughts back to Pippy, one of the dogs that I have loved so much. Thanks to his compassionate gaze into my eyes, Pippy helped remove some of the pain I was carrying in my heart caused by my mother's death. Pippy connected with me in a profound way that wasn't human, but was creature to creature.

In the new heavens and the new earth, and in the "Peaceable Kingdom" described by the prophet Isaiah, the lion and the lamb and many other creatures live together in happy harmony. One of the themes of this book is that the whole family of creation is meant to walk together in peace and harmony on this earth as we journey to God. I found

Pippy helpful in my own life's journey, in that he made my mother's death easier to bear. Of course, many loving human beings also consoled me in similar ways through their prayers, words, and loving support. Yet, it is consoling to remember that our animal companions are also able to support us in such stressful situations.

There is another image from Revelation that follows immediately after John's vision of "a new heaven and a new earth," and that is the "new Jerusalem."

John writes: "I also saw the holy city, the new Jerusalem, coming down out of heaven from God, prepared as a bride adorned for her husband. I heard a loud voice from the throne saying, 'Behold, God's dwelling is with the human race. He will dwell with them and they will be his people and God himself will always be with them (as their God)'" (Rev. 21:2–3 NAB). This, too, has implications for our hope that we will see our pets in heaven.

The idea expresses an amazingly intense and loving, marriagelike union between God and his people. This intimate union would be a state of happiness not unlike heaven itself. In fact, if we were to die in that kind of union with God, we would indeed be in heaven.

Even now, if we are trying to live our lives out of love for God and according to God's plan, we would be enjoying a heavenlike state, would we not?—or at least a *foretaste* of the heaven still to come?

After announcing, through John, this kind of union between God and the human race, "The one who sat on the throne said, 'Behold, I make all things new'" (Rev. 21:5 NAB). God seems to be going well beyond making all human beings new to say "I make *all things* new." *All things* is the literal translation of the Greek word *panta*. The word is clearly neuter and would refer to all things of creation taken together, including human, animal, plant, and mineral.

The Jerusalem Bible translation is: "Now I am making the whole of creation new." God's saving love includes the whole family of creation, not only the human beings.

14
Conclusion

Jesus once said that we are to have faith like children. Kids can sometimes see and understand those things that we adults, for whatever reasons, no longer seem to see or understand quite as clearly.

Many people whose pets have died have personally told me that they just "know" in their hearts or by some inner intuition that their beloved dog or cat or parrot is in heaven. Children often have a similar instinct or inner sense about their pets and other animals being in heaven.

Jesus once uttered this prayer: "I bless you, Father, Lord of heaven and of earth, for hiding these things from the learned and the clever and revealing them to mere children" (Mt. 11:25 JB). In this spirit, I have something similar to share with you. . . .

Thanks to the kind assistance of a friend, an elementary school teacher in Cincinnati, eight first-grade students offered these brief answers to my question:

"Why should animals go to heaven?"

1. "If they didn't go to heaven, who would take care of them?" (Jackson)

2. "So they can be with their owner who loves them." (Liz)

3. "Because it's the only place for them to go if they are good." (Jakari)

4. "Because they are good." (Nathan)

5. "Because God loves his creations." (Leah)

6. "Because he [God] loves them and wants them to live with him." (Amber)

7. "When it dies, where else would it go?" (Rachel)

8. "If only *people* were in heaven, it would be boring." (Radu)

We may not know exactly how God will bring the whole family of creation some day to heaven. What we do know is this: our faith, supported by Scripture, Christian teaching, and the life and example of St. Francis of Assisi, gives us solid hints and clues that if we live in harmony with God's plans, we will see the "whole of creation" in the world to come.

Does our most holy and good Creator-God need our permission to fill his new heaven and new earth with the whole family of creation? Of course not. Nor did God need our permission to place them in that first primeval Paradise.

This gift of life with God in a new heaven and a new earth comes simply from God's own overflowing love and goodness. What is more, in this restored garden-still-to-come there will be no wall of separation between the holy and the profane, the sacred and the secular. That wall is one that *we* make, and, of course, it does not exist in the eyes of God. In heaven, the holiness of all God's creatures will be apparent. Even though all of us earthly creatures are clearly distinct from God, we will yet, somehow, be one with God and the risen Jesus. "[God] is not far from each one of us," as St. Paul reminded the Athenians. "For 'in him we live and move and have our being'" (Acts 17:27–28).

In the new heaven and new earth God will walk side by side with all of us. "The wolf shall be the guest of the lamb" (Isa. 11:6 NAB), and, hopefully, the fox will live with the rabbit, and we humans will be the happy companions and loving caregivers of our dogs and cats—and all the other creatures.

I have come to believe, "Yes, with heartfelt thanks to God's saving love for the whole family of creation, *I will see my dog in heaven!*"

About Paraclete Press

Who We Are

Paraclete Press is a publisher of books, recordings, and DVDs on Christian spirituality. Our publishing represents a full expression of Christian belief and practice—from Catholic to Evangelical, from Protestant to Orthodox.

We are the publishing arm of the Community of Jesus, an ecumenical monastic community in the Benedictine tradition. As such, we are uniquely positioned in the marketplace without connection to a large corporation and with informal relationships to many branches and denominations of faith.

What We Are Doing

Books | Paraclete publishes books that show the richness and depth of what it means to be Christian. Although Benedictine spirituality is at the heart of all that we do, we publish books that reflect the Christian experience across many cultures, time periods, and houses of worship. We publish books that nourish the vibrant life of the church and its people—books about spiritual practice, formation, history, ideas, and customs.

We have several different series, including the best-selling Living Library, Paraclete Essentials, and Paraclete Giants series of classic texts in contemporary English; A Voice from the Monastery—men and women monastics writing about living a spiritual life today; award-winning literary faith fiction and poetry; and the Active Prayer Series that brings creativity and liveliness to any life of prayer.

Recordings | From Gregorian chant to contemporary American choral works, our music recordings celebrate sacred choral music through the centuries. Paraclete distributes the recordings of the internationally acclaimed choir Gloriæ Dei Cantores, praised for their "rapt and fathomless spiritual intensity" by *American Record Guide*, and the Gloriæ Dei Cantores Schola, which specializes in the study and performance of Gregorian chant. Paraclete is also the exclusive North American distributor of the recordings of the Monastic Choir of St. Peter's Abbey in Solesmes, France, long considered to be a leading authority on Gregorian chant.

DVDs | Our DVDs offer spiritual help, healing, and biblical guidance for life issues: grief and loss, marriage, forgiveness, anger management, facing death, and spiritual formation.

Learn more about us at our website:www.paracletepress.com,
or call us toll-free at 1-800-451-5006.

You may also be interested in …

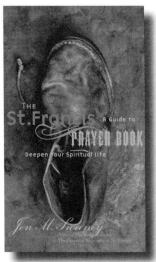

The St. Francis Prayer Book

A Guide to Deepen Your Spiritual Life

Jon M. Sweeney

ISBN 978-1-55725-352-1 | $14.99, Paperback

This warm-hearted little book is a window into the soul of St. Francis, one of the most passionate and inspiring followers of Jesus. With this guide, readers will:

- Pray the words that Francis taught his spiritual brothers and sisters to pray.
- Explore Francis's time and place and feel the joy and earnestness of the first Franciscans.
- Experience how it is possible to live a contemplative and active life, at the same time.

Available from most booksellers or through Paraclete Press

www.paracletepress.com   •   1-800-451-5006

Try your local bookstore first